SCOTLAND'S
CINEMAS

PHOTOGRAPHS

Lily Publications

SCOTLAND'S CINEMAS

BRUCE PETER

ISBN: 978-1-907945-05-2

Published by:
Lily Publications Ltd
PO Box 33
Ramsey
Isle of Man
IM99 4LP

This first edition © Lily Publications Ltd 2011.

www.lilypublications.co.uk

Typeset in Eric Gill's Perpetua and Gill Sans

CONTENTS

SCOTLAND'S CINEMAS

Acknowledgements

My especial thanks are given to David Parsons for copy editing the manuscript, Ian Smith for devising the page layouts and Miles Cowsill for publishing the work.

My thanks are given to: Aberdeen Central Library, Aberdeen Picture Palaces, The Architectural Heritage Society of Scotland, Louis Barfe, Gordon Barr, Bill Beattie, Marion Beveridge, Patrick Brader, William Brogden, Jim Brooks, Ian Bruce, Alex Cameron, Edmund Campbell, Forbes Castell, The Cinema Theatre Association, Roger Clarke, Paul Connolly, Paddy Cronin of McMillan & Cronin, Ian Cunningham, Chris Doak, John Donald, John Duddy, John Earl, Allen Eyles, John Fairley, Elizabeth Ferguson, Archie Foley, June Forsyth, Robert Forsyth, Vincent Gillen of The Greenock Museum, Glasgow City Archives, Kevin Gooding, Govan Reminiscence Group, Richard Gray, Tommy Green, Forsyth Hardy, Margaret Hardy, Elain Harwood, Xandra Harper, Geoffrey Jarvis, Juliet Kinchin, George Lane, Janet McBain, Barney McCue, Scott McCutcheon, Charles McKean, John J. McKillop, H.S. McNair, Robin McSkimming, Liana Marletta, Mecca Bingo staff, Ann Menzies, George Miller, Ian Miller, Margeorie Meekie, the late Tony Moss, Brian Oakaby, Nicholas Oddy, Robert Palmer, Gary Painter, John Peter, Baajie Pickard, Ian Ramsay, Barry Roberts, The Rev Archie and Mrs Robertson, Gaylie Runciman, Adrienne Scullion, John Sheeran, Tommy Sinclair, George and Ronald Singleton, Robbie Smith, Stephen Smith, Gari Todd, Springburn Museum, Richard Stenlake, Andrew Stuart, The Theatres Trust, Gertie and Trixie Thomson, David Trevor-Jones, John Urie, Stafford Waters, Robin Webster, Tom Weir, Kevin Wheelan and Alastair White.

Introduction

THE experience of modernity and modern life in the rapidly expanding cities of the latter 19th century was one of constant flux and movement – an unprecedented maelstrom of traffic and pedestrians, mingling with the nascent signs of consumerism, represented in bold electric lighting. For populations who had hitherto been rural-dwelling, the shock of this new environment must have been all the more profound. Furthermore, the regulation of time in the workplace led workers to prize their 'quality time' of leisure hours all the more. A consequence of these phenomena was the increasing desire for stimuli to match or outdo those of the everyday city. Thus, mass-spectator sports grew rapidly in popularity, as did such fairground attractions as the roller-coaster. It seems that the public wanted to extract the maximum possible sensation from every free moment. People knew, however, that such moments would pass quickly and that a return to the daily grind was inevitable – a fact that only redoubled the desires of thrill-seekers to search for the latest and most stimulating diversions. This situation both precipitated and ran in parallel with the rapid growth of the cinema industry.

Since the Industrial Revolution, design for pleasure has directly addressed popular taste, which is multifaceted, constantly evolving, difficult to predict and hard to quantify until the 'moment' has passed. 'Serious' architecture, on the other hand, usually evolves slowly and so 'mainstream' architectural discourse, representing high culture, almost always attempts to bring about buildings that stand the test of time and aspire to a significance outlasting passing fads. Yet, as architecture and design historians know, it is often buildings that speak most strongly of their period by exhibiting recognisable stylistic traits that are the most enduringly popular and successful. Cinemas are interesting and important, therefore, because perhaps more than any other building type, they were designed to try to capture the fashion of the moment and, as we shall see, their designs often contained complex, but deliberately selected, stylistic nuances borrowed from a wide range of influences.

The nature of the cinema architecture – creating places where indulgence is a virtue – can be seen as part of a long-standing utopian tradition of leisure at the centre of life. In 1946, George Orwell observed of leisure in the 1930s that:

> 'The modern civilised man's idea of pleasure is already partly attained in the more magnificent dance halls, movie palaces, hotels, restaurants and luxury liners. On a pleasure cruise or in a Lyons Corner House one already gets something more than a glimpse of this future paradise.'

The alternative world conjured up by the new entertainment venues, however, was actually rooted in material reality and had its origins in the new patterns of work in the 19th century. In all this, work assumed not simply a more dominant role on account of the great number of hours it demanded, but it also gave rise to its own ethic to legitimise the sacrifices required and to the concept of 'honest labour' because a reliable, available labour force was a key component of the whole process.

The work was often, at best, dull and, at worst, dangerous. Reformers achieved gradual success in whittling away at the number of hours worked and, in the space that was freed, leisure time emerged to generate its own distinctive patterns of activity. What to do with this time has become a question of growing social

Above: The entrance to the Picture Palace, Ayr (1911) is in the centre of this pre-First World War view. Typically of early cinemas, the entrance is brightly painted – cleanliness symbolising modernity and respectability. (Bruce Peter collection)

Below left: Crouch's Wonderland (1881) was a small music hall in Glasgow's Argyle Street which added Cinematograph to its programmes in the latter-1890s. It was subsequently re-built as the St Enoch Picture Theatre (1913). (Bruce Peter collection)

Below right: The BB Cinerama (J. Campbell Reid, 1912) in Victoria Road on Glasgow's South Side was converted from a roller skating rink. (Bruce Peter collection)

Bottom right: The entrance to the Theatre de Luxe in Glasgow's Sauchiehall Street – a typical city centre cinema of the Edwardian era, entered through a shop unit. (Bruce Peter collection)

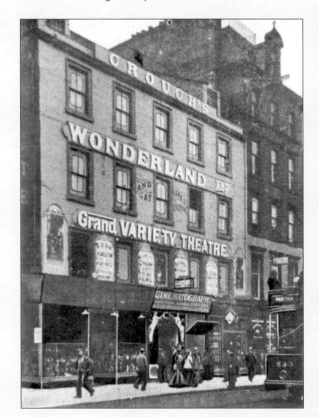

importance. In spite of its inherent attractiveness, and the fact that it has been the dream of generations, leisure was now seen to pose its own problems. Not the least of these problems was the fact that 'leisure time' was the remaining space left by work, and subject to the same structural pressures and constraints as work itself. In spite of its promise of escapism, leisure remained inescapably a part of industrial society and so entertainment for the masses came to be provided on an industrial scale.

In Scotland, film exhibition developed apace from primitive travelling shows, setting up wherever they could find a suitable space, to technically sophisticated performances in comfortable, efficient venues, many of which were notable examples of a prolific and fascinating architectural genre. This trend was accelerated by an Act of Parliament. In the early days film shows could be given almost anywhere and there were almost no safety regulations. The risk of fire, in particular, was very high. Public concern about picture-house safety mounted and the British Government quickly introduced the Kinematograph Act of 1909, which demanded certain basic safety standards such as fireproof projection booths, adequate exits and local authority inspection and licensing of cinema premises. The first generation of properly planned conversions and purpose-built cinemas emerged to take account of the new regulations. From then on competition for the growing and increasingly enthusiastic cinema-going public was fierce and it spawned the remarkable number and diversity of cinemas, explored in the following chapters.

The first post-Kinematograph Act generation of converted and purpose-built cinemas was undoubtedly basic, but luxurious 'picture palaces' soon began to appear which could rival the finest anywhere in Europe. However, the advent of the First World War brought about an abrupt halt to construction, which did not resume until after the 1918 armistice. While Britain had been fighting, the Americans had been perfecting not only the art of making movies but also of designing and building cinemas, and so many of the grandest Scottish cinemas of the 1920s were modelled on American precedents. Indeed, some cinema architects, such as John Fairweather, even travelled to the United States to examine the latest American design principles. The late-twenties saw the advent of 'atmospheric' cinemas – also based on American ideas – such as the Toledo at Muirend, the Boulevard in Knightswood and the Orient

in the Gallowgate (all located around Glasgow). Their auditoria were embellished with stucco buildings and their ceilings painted or lit to give their audiences the illusion of being in romantic and exotic courtyards under dark, starry skies.

The introduction of sound to movies put a large number of smaller, more primitive picture-houses out of business. Talkie apparatus was expensive and the new generation of more comfortable and efficient cinemas that emerged around the same time made the competition tougher than ever.

This innovation was paralleled by new developments in architecture and interior design in Germany and France during the decade following the First World War. Progressive German commercial architecture was characterised mainly by expressionism – which emphasised dynamic forms and bold night illumination to make consumerism exciting for shoppers and entertainment-seekers. The Berlin architect Eric Mendelsohn was a leading exponent of the aesthetic and there he designed several large department stores and also the Universum cinema, completed in 1928. With the rise of Nazism in Germany, Mendelsohn, who was a Jew, fled to Britain where he subsequently won an architectural competition to design a new seaside pavilion

The façade of the Govan Cinema (Richard Henderson, 1913) perhaps shows the influence of Glasgow's great exhibitions in 1888 and 1901. This was an early member of the SCVT (later ABC) cinema circuit and was replaced by ABC's Plaza super cinema in the mid-1930s. (Bruce Peter collection)

The Mecca, Possilpark, Glasgow (James McKissack, 1933) served a new Corporation housing scheme. (Bruce Peter collection)

Left and above: The Mecca's interior was in the then-fashionable 'jazz moderne' manner, as these illustrations of a side exit door and the proscenium show. (Bruce Peter collection)

Above left and right: The Regent, Aberdeen (1932) was a member of the Edinburgh-based Poole circuit. Again, this showed jazz moderne overtones. Later in the 1930s, the angular shapes slipped from fashion when streamlining became all the rage.
(Bruce Peter collection)

at Bexhill-on-Sea, the De La Warr Pavilion completed in 1935. It proved highly influential as an inspiration for British public buildings during the latter 1930s.

Partially in response to German progressive developments in architecture, technology and the decorative arts, in 1925 France attempted to re-assert its authority as the pre-eminent international style leader for *haute couture* and luxury goods design and production by staging a showcase international exhibition in the heart of Paris, around the Eiffel Tower. The *Exposition des Arts Décoratifs et Industriels Modernes* has passed into legend as the progenitor of what is today known as the Art Deco style. The exhibition, however, was heavily politicised and Germany, France's main rival in the manufacture of all that was modern and desirable, pointedly was not invited to be represented. As Britain had staged its own Empire Exhibition at Wembley in London the previous year, its exhibit was only perfunctory. America, on the other hand, claimed that, as it copied all of its 'high end' design output from European precedents, it would have nothing original to contribute – an ironic situation indeed, given that increasing numbers of European architects were, at that very moment, trooping to America in droves to marvel at Manhattan skyscrapers and the chaser lights and billboard advertisements of Times Square.

For the most part, the Paris *Exposition* showcased lavish and highly crafted French couture design, with an emphasis upon interiors and fashion, all of which utilised very expensive materials and aesthetics rooted in the Rococo, mixed with elements of Art Nouveau and an eclectic mix of French colonial styles from North and West Africa, French Indo-China and Central America. French Art Deco, as it emerged during the 1920s, was

very luxurious and it became highly desirable amongst the fashionable set on both sides of the Atlantic – and elsewhere. Two years after the Paris *Exposition*, the brand-new French trans-Atlantic liner *Ile de France* made her maiden voyage from Le Havre to New York, bringing the *Exposition*'s high style to the United States. Shortly thereafter, American hotel interiors, skyscrapers and film sets adopted the look and, through the movies, the style was emulated all over the world. Indeed, in somewhat debased form, it inspired the design of countless cinemas during the 1930s – not least in Scotland. In its more popular and commercial forms, Art Deco also was influenced by the syncopated rhythms of jazz music – leading to designs featuring repeated zig-zag, wave and 'sunburst' patterns – a style of decoration known as 'jazz moderne'. This was hated by architecture critics, but loved by consumers because it was bright, modern and obviously signalled enjoyment. In many cinemas, a variety of fashionably modern design styles were freely mixed together – and this eclectic approach only served further to incense critics who evidently associated design purity with virtue, a dubious belief but one still widely held within the architectural community.

During the 1930s, the quest for speed – fast trains, aircraft and Blue Riband-winning trans-Atlantic ocean liners – was reflected in commercial architecture and so buildings of various kinds came increasingly to be streamlined. As the decade progressed, the symmetrical

The Playhouse, Stornoway mixes jazz moderne and Scottish vernacular elements, as this 1950s image demonstrates. (George Millar)

Very occasionally, cinemas were discreetly fitted into the existing townscape – usually because their owners could not find a site enabling an impressive street frontage to be built. Such a case was the Argosy, Bucksburn. (Gary Painter collection)

A Glasgow Corporation 'Coronation'-type tram passes the Cinema, Coatbridge (1913), which has a prominent asbestos cement roof. (Bruce Peter collection)

The rather eccentric New Alex, Paisley (A.V. Gardner, 1923)makes its presence felt in this pre-war image of Neilston Road. (Bruce Peter collection)

Green's Playhouse, Dundee (John Fairweather and Joseph Emberton, 1936) had the tallest tower of any cinema in Britain – a very distinctive landmark on the city's Nethergate. (Bruce Peter collection)

Various styles of twentieth century commercial buildings in Falkirk: the moderne Regal cinema (McNair & Elder, 1934) nestles between Art Nouveau, neo-Tudor and neo-classical frontages. (Bruce Peter collection)

The shock of the new: the extraordinary Radio cinema in Kilbirnie, complete with pseudo transmission mast (James Houston, 1937). (Bruce Peter collection)

geometric forms inspired by the Paris *Exposition* were superseded by façade and interior designs emphasising smoothness, rounded corners, elongated horizontal and soaring vertical accents. In Glasgow, Thomas Tait and a group of other moderately progressive architects designed the 1938 Empire Exhibition in Bellahouston Park in this manner. Simultaneously, sleek tiled 'super' cinemas, boldly outlined at night in vividly coloured neon, appeared on the main arterial roads of Scotland's larger towns and cities, their advertising hoardings carefully placed to attract the attention of passing tram passengers. A greater contrast to the grimy ashlar-faced tenements whose street scene they shared would be hard to imagine.

For many urban Scots there were at least two cinemas within ten minutes' walk of home. In some areas rival cinemas stood so close together that children queuing for matinées would be bribed with free sticks of rock by one manager and with free balloons by another. People from every social class and all walks of life went to the cinema, from those who arrived at sumptuous 'super' cinemas by automobile to the urban poor who queued in shoals at sordid halls where children would urinate on the floor. Cinemas fulfilled a vital social function. They were great public lounges in which couples courted, friendships were made, gossip was exchanged, fights were fought, babies were born and the elderly passed away. The manager often knew all his regular customers and would take time to chat with patrons and happily arrange special events. In working class areas the local cinema provided warmth, relative comfort and much-needed recreational space, particularly during the Depression when taking the family to the pictures was often cheaper than keeping the fire and the lights on at home.

Even smaller communities — such as Anstruther, Newport-on-Tay and Auchterarder — could support a cinema and some remarkable designs appeared during the 1930s. Many attempted to evoke the glamour of the largest city centre houses — albeit ingeniously scaled down. Such rural cinemas often served large farming hinterlands and were particular attractions on market day.

Architecturally, however, cinemas were controversial. Aspiring modernist architects and critics condemned them for their flashy façades, poorly finished rear quarters and lack of sympathy towards the existing townscape and found their gaudiness and blatant self-advertisement distasteful, perhaps not realising that a reticent cinema

would be a contradiction in terms. As a genre, the cinema had the potential to be an archetypal modernist project in terms of its reproducibility, its use of technology, its potential to inform and educate and its possible use of avant-garde graphic design, photography techniques and scenography. From the perspective of the 'true' modernist, the fact that it continually appeared to be debased and made 'modernistic' to attract mass audiences was problematic and this tied into wider debates about high and mass culture.

Those on the left came to believe that mass culture was merely an opiate for the masses created on an industrial scale by the entertainment industry to keep the working classes happy and at a lower cultural level to prevent the fermentation of revolution. From a Marxist perspective, it appeared that mass entertainment had a similar effect of social control to religion in that a relatively small élite controlled what was to be indulged in by the masses. Nor did the idea of mass entertainment find favour with right-wingers, for whom nostalgia and conservatism encouraged a backward look to a model of folk culture that had been all but swept away by the tide of industrialisation. The recreation of the masses was seen less as indigenous and more as an imposed culture with the word 'popular' actually being a polite pseudonym meaning 'coarse' and 'inferior'.

Notwithstanding, cinema architecture evolved as a large (and highly lucrative) specialist genre unto itself. However, auditorium design represented a very specific architectural problem concerning the supporting structure for balconies, optimising sight-lines, acoustics and audience safety concerns. It was no surprise that the vast majority of cinema buildings were the work of highly skilled specialists who rarely designed anything else. The Kinematograph Act ensured that the source of film projection was situated outwith the cinema auditorium in a separately accessed booth and that there was a solid wall between with glazed portholes and steel fire shutters. The other main requirement was for adequate audience escape routes, solid partition walls with fire doors and rudimentary fire-fighting equipment. So, for reasons of safety, cinemas were highly compartmentalised buildings which would never have been able to satisfy Le Corbusier's demand for *Plan Libre*. From there being almost no purpose-built cinemas at the time of the Kinematograph Act, there were over 5,000 throughout Britain by the time of the Second World War — an unprecedented expansion in entertainment provision. Cinemas stood sentinel on almost every high street throughout Britain and, for better or worse, they were too prominent to be ignored or dismissed. Scotland had many fine examples and in 1939 the average Scot went to the pictures 35 times a year whereas the English average was only 21 visits – amazing, given that so many Scots lived in rural communities. The story of their design evolution is a rich and fascinating one.

Cinema architecture had its own commercial logic and, as the cinema had an important role to play in society, it required to be judged against its own criteria. Cinema architects clearly understood the need to advertise and the ability of modern design and construction methods to 'sell' an attraction was a bonus. For financiers, architects, designers and builders, entertainment was a serious business, and so cinemas needed to appeal very directly to potential customers. The influences of different owners, developers and architects, each with their own vision of what would attract custom, initially brought about a remarkable diversity of design solutions. By the late-1930s, however, a universal language had been developed. Positively seductive imagery – bright, clean colours, soaring towers, bold neon-outlined graphics in modern fonts,

smooth lines, curved corners, fins and ocean liner motifs – helped to emphasise the cinema's modernity, slickness, efficiency and glamour. Notwithstanding the pressures of time and finance, in the main architects used much flair and imagination in designing these highly regulated structures. (That does not excuse the many badly proportioned and shoddily designed edifices which undoubtedly also existed.) Moreover, the taste of the public was erratic, and so extremes of purity were usually deliberately avoided anyway, especially in buildings intended to attract 'mainstream' audiences.

The vast majority of the cinemas referred to have either been demolished or significantly altered, while only a few remain in pristine condition, and so this book provides a record of many lost buildings. That so many of the best surviving cinemas are now listed buildings shows that for them the cycle of taste has come full-circle and that they have at last come to be seen as culturally and historically significant. However, for a curious and entertainment-hungry public, Scotland's cinemas directly addressed the need for spiritual uplift during difficult periods – between the Great Depression and the Second World War and during the post-war austerity phase. The 1930s super cinema was at the progressive end of popular taste and exemplified modern architecture for the masses.

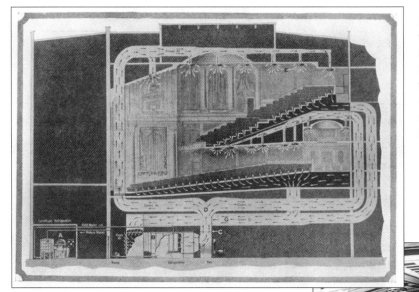

Left: Cinemas were complex buildings with highly compartmentalised layouts and a great deal of hidden servicing fitted into void spaces between the auditorium floor, walls and ceiling and the buildings' exterior cladding. This sectional drawing shows the workings of the ventilation system in a typical super cinema of the 1930s. (Bruce Peter collection)

Right: What the public saw: the auditorium of the Rialto, Kirkcaldy (1924) with bright paintwork and murals on the side walls helping to create a popular impression of luxury. (Bruce Peter collection)

The First Picture Shows

THE French inventors Claude and Auguste Lumière presented the first British cinema show on 20 February 1896 in the Great Hall of the Regent Street Polytechnic (now part of the University of London). The Lumières intended their invention more as a significant scientific invention than a means of entertainment, an attitude entirely in keeping with Victorian values. The invention of the moving picture was perceived as one of the crowning ambitions of man, and serious scientific research was then taking place into the very nature of movement. It was, however, the travelling show and variety impresarios who first exploited the possibilities of showing cinema reels for entertainment.

Film first reached Scotland via Edison's Kinetoscope peep-shows which had their earliest recorded appearance at H.E. Moss' Christmas Carnival at the Waverley Market in Edinburgh on 24 December 1894. Moss' lifespan (1852-1912) parallels the development of the popular entertainment industry during the Victorian and Edwardian eras. His father, James Moss, had initially been a travelling showman, before converting the Mechanics' Institute in Greenock into the Lorne Music Hall, which he then managed. Thus, his son H. E. Moss was born into the variety business. In 1877 he acquired his own music hall, the Gaiety in Chambers Street, Edinburgh, and he subsequently built up a substantial chain of ever-larger and more opulent variety theatres located in Glasgow, Edinburgh, Newcastle and other industrial centres. With a burgeoning and profitable business and a well-established infrastructure necessary to promote touring variety shows, Moss was a particularly influential and innovative force in the development of cinema in its early years.

Moving pictures using Lumière equipment first achieved notice as part of a variety bill on 13 April 1896 at Moss' **Empire Palace** in Nicholson Street, Edinburgh. The event was enticingly billed in *The Scotsman* as 'The Cinematographe....The greatest novelty of the Age...The latest scientific triumph, showing animated pictures. The rage of London and Paris.' However, on 14 April the same newspaper's review of the first night of what was a week-long engagement indicates that it was by no means an overnight success:

'The great advertised attraction for this week at the Empire is an exhibition of the 'Cinematographe' – a kind of electric magic lantern by which the instantaneous photographs of Edison's wonderful Kinetoscope are thrown upon a screen in sight of the audience. The Cinematographe has been a great success at the London Empire, and Mr Moss is to be complimented for his enterprise in securing the first appearance of it in the provinces. Unfortunately, in Edinburgh last night the exhibition somehow misfired. These instantaneous photographs are, it may be recalled, printed on a celluloid ribbon, which... was made to fly across the lens by means of an electric motor...In the Cinematographe... the light seemed not to be powerful enough to render the celluloid sufficiently transparent, and a somewhat indistinct picture in consequence appeared on the screen – such as might have been thrown if the instrument had not been properly focused. Another defect was that the photographs were passed too slowly before the lens so that... the dancing and pugilistic scenes especially (were) of too funereal a character. It was noticed that the lighter photographs showed best upon the screen. Such, for example, was 'The Shoeblack, the Policeman

SCOTLAND'S CINEMAS

Above left: A sketch of the Ice Skating Palace, Glasgow. It is interesting to compare this image with a subsequent photograph of the same building after re-building as the Regal cinema, shown on page 77. (Scottish Screen Archive)

Above right: The showman and cinema pioneer Arthur Hubner. (CTA Archive)

Below: The Empire Palace Theatre, Edinburgh (Frank Matcham, 1892) – the venue of Scotland's first public cinema show. Note the large auditorium block barely hidden from view by two-storey shop units. (Bruce Peter collection)

and the Sailor', which was the first and best of the ten scenes exhibited. 'The Cockfight' was also exceedingly good, the action of the birds flying at each other with outstretched wings being very realistic. Mr T. Moore Howard, who showed the scenes, apologised for the hitches which had occurred, but claimed at the same time the indulgence of the audience on the ground that the Cinematographe was only in its infancy, and that it would take several months yet to perfect. There are, unquestionably, great possibilities in this interesting, scientific toy, if it may be so called, and when it is perfected the Empire audience will no doubt be glad to see it all again…'

The venue of that first faltering Scottish cinema performance had staged its first show of any kind in November 1892 and was in itself an amazing building – it being a veritable multi-purpose entertainment palace. The Victorians were obsessed with horse racing and the British Empire now embraced all sorts of countries with many species of exotic animals. A new style of 'Empire' entertainment was in the making. Frank Matcham, acknowledged as Britain's greatest Victorian theatre architect, expressed these ideals by designing for Moss the largest, best equipped theatre in the country. Apart from its massive 3,000 capacity, his design incorporated many innovations. Although the Empire Palace's street frontage was narrow, the venue was strategically located on a busy section of Nicholson Street – close to Waverley Railway Station and adjacent to the University. To attract attention, Matcham devised a flamboyant gilded oriental tower with a copper onion dome surmounted by a life-size female figure – certainly it was conspicuous! This was but a foretaste of the wonders housed within. The auditorium was huge with three well-spaced galleries, all supported by cantilevers and smothered in ornate fibrous plasterwork. The height of the auditorium was designed to take into account sight-lines for aerial trapeze acts. There was a sliding roof for ventilation (essential if up to three performances a day were to take place). The stage was claimed to be the most flexible in the country as the entire proscenium arch could be folded away to accommodate circus acts; meanwhile the stage divided into modules which quickly retracted to reveal a circus ring underneath. So successful was the arrangement that it was possible to present a complete circus in the afternoon and variety the same evening.

Only six weeks later, on 26 May 1896, the Cinematographe received its première in Glasgow in another remarkable entertainment building – **The Ice Skating Palace** at 326 Sauchiehall Street. Until the 1870s cattle had grazed in fields around Garnethill but by 1882 the area was sufficiently urban to attract the Diorama, an octagonal-shaped hall which displayed large canvases of famous myths and historical events. For the 1888 International Exhibition the Diorama was converted into the Panorama, a more advanced type of spectacle in which dramatic paintings on rolls of canvas were wound across a proscenium – a forerunner of moving pictures on film. A series depicting the Battle of Bannockburn, painted by Professor Fleischer of Munich, was a great favourite and The Battle of Trafalgar, The Battle of Waterloo and The Battle of Omdurman were all major successes: the 1880s equivalent of epic movies. Later, in 1885, it was converted for ice skating at the height of that craze. It contained a single horseshoe-shaped balcony surrounding the ice rink to enable spectators to view ice dancing shows in relative comfort. When this waned, its managing director, Major Tyre, struggled to find an audience. He employed Arthur Hubner, a South African-born music hall entrepreneur, to try to revive its fortunes. An important figure in the early development of cinema in Glasgow, Hubner was one of the first to realise the financial possibilities of regular film performances and from then on included films in all his shows at the Ice Skating Palace – which was temporarily converted into a variety hall. There the Lumière Cinematographe was again used but press reaction was more enthusiastic than it had been in Edinburgh. *The Quiz* (28 May 1896) reported that:

'The Managers of the Skating Palace are determined to be up-to-date. On Tuesday night they introduced to a Glasgow audience for the first time, the Cinematographe. The fame that has preceded this latest wonder was the means of drawing an exceptionally large gathering, who were all well repaid for their attendance. The Cinematographe consists of a series of snap-shot photos taken at a rate of 900 per minute, shown on a screen. The series enlarged, following each other with such rapidity, that they form one scene with the life fully portrayed. Seven pictures were shown, one being a lady performing the 'Skirt Dance.' A London street scene followed; 'buses,

Jamaica Street in Glasgow in the 1890s with Walter Wilson's Colosseum warehouse on the left-hand side. (Bruce Peter collection)

carriages, pedestrians are fully portrayed. You see a carriage or a 'bus come dashing up, horses prancing, and people skipping across the street. A bridge with the people and traffic crossing proved highly entertaining, especially the gentleman with the light overcoat, and a lady by his side. A blacksmith's shop with the men all hard at work; the steam rising from the water when the hot iron was plunged in, proved very effective; the train arriving at the station, passengers alighting, and the lady rushing along the platform to meet her friend, was very amusing; the sea shore, with the waves breaking on the beach, brought the exhibition to a close, amid the loud applause of the audience. Altogether, the latest invention of the age proved a decided success, and it is sure to attract large crowds to the Palace…'

Unfortunately, performance of the Cinematographe later that week only attracted meagre audiences relative to the size of the venue. Perhaps this was because they were held too late in the evening, by which time those looking for entertainment in the city centre would already have been ensconced in rival theatres and music halls.

By early 1897 Hubner must have done some market research. He started showing specially-made films of local interest. *The Departure of the Columba from Rothesay Pier* honoured the famous Clyde steamer and *The Gordon Highlanders Leaving Maryhill Barracks* doubtless aroused patriotic pride as the kilted soldiers marched (probably at a ridiculous speed) down Maryhill Road. The programme was a triumph for Hubner and ran at the Ice Skating Palace for months.

Hubner must be credited with realising the entertainment potential of film, as distinct from film as scientific-novelty as it had generally been perceived. He was successful despite the fact that the Ice Skating Palace proved ultimately to be a wholly inappropriate venue with poor acoustics and an auditorium with sight-lines focused on the ice arena rather than the temporary cinema screen. In 1897, as we shall see, he transferred his business to the **Britannia Music Hall** in the city's Trongate where he again implemented a cine-variety policy. Film shows began to look as though they might have serious business potential and other showmen and entrepreneurs were not long in getting in on the act.

Walter Wilson had set up Edison's Kinetoscope in his **Colosseum** Warehouse, a department store in Jamaica Street, during the 1895 Christmas holidays. Wilson was an ambitious man with diverse business interests. In addition to owning the Colosseum he was the main supplier of limelight and other equipment to Glasgow theatres and music halls. Never one to miss an opportunity, he was inspired by the popularity of his Kinetoscope, and by Hubner's success, to set up a 500 seat cinema in the Colosseum. He heralded its opening, on 30 November 1896, with newspaper advertisements proclaiming:

'This extraordinary invention is the marvel of the age. Every picture is full of life. The following realistic scenes may be seen at every exhibition of the Kinematograph – the English Channel at Dover: the Ostend steamer and the Calais mail steamer are seen to sail away until lost in the distance; Scenes of everyday life on the boulevards of Paris; An animated railway station scene; A funny comedy called 'Two Strings To Her Bow'; The Czar in Paris. Admission 3d.'

The hesitant were advised 'if you have not seen the Kinematograph, you are behind the age', a challenge bound to get a response from the venturesome and forward-looking Glaswegians. Although it still relied on Lumière material, Wilson's show was a great success.

Aberdeen's first cinema show, again using Lumière equipment, took place on 28 September 1896 in the **Alhambra**, located close to the harbour and the main railway station on the corner of Guild and Exchange Streets. It had been converted to a music hall in 1881 from the Trinity Chapel of Ease (known locally as the 'Tarty Kirk'). It was run by the Livermore brothers, who were important North East variety impresarios (they also ran the city's Palace Theatre) as a 'try out' venue for new talent. Unfortunately, the upmarket Palace burned down two days after the Alhambra's pioneering cinema show, and so the Livermore brothers were forced to make it into their main venue while the Palace was re-built. During the ensuing period, cinematograph shows became

a popular feature of the Alhambra's variety bills. Once the Palace re-opened, the Alhambra housed a waxworks and a menagerie. Later, from 1907, it was leased to an animal trainer called John Sinclair, who owned a small summer zoo by the beach. Sinclair decided to make his attraction all-year-round, and so the Alhambra became his 'Winter Zoo', again with popular cinema shows as an extra. The Alhambra's end came in May 1910 but the building still exists as a Chinese restaurant and shop.

Cinema's popularity, and its respectability, were greatly enhanced by Queen Victoria's Diamond Jubilee in 1897. It was a spectacular opportunity for the cinematograph and film of the event became the first newsreel in Britain. It aroused immense interest around the country and, in Glasgow, was shown in no less grand a venue than the Fine Art Institute in Glasgow's Sauchiehall Street. Variety theatres throughout Scotland cashed in on the excitement by including films among their attractions.

In the final years of the nineteenth century, with the cinematograph increasingly and widely available, the screening of film became a key element in the programmes of many variety halls. Moss' **Empire Palace Theatre** in Glasgow's Sauchiehall Street was one of the venues that most consistently acquired films for its patrons. The theatre, which opened in April 1897, was built on the site of an older music hall, the Gaiety, which had been demolished the previous year. As with the Edinburgh Empire Palace, Moss put the design of the new theatre in the capable hands of Frank Matcham. Whereas in Edinburgh Matcham had to make the most of a cramped site, here he had two long frontages at one of Glasgow's busiest street junctions. As ever, he rose to the occasion with vigour. The four-storey edifice was finished in red sandstone, boldly carved in Italian Renaissance style but topped by soaring Indian minarets. Within, the foyer (for stalls and circle patrons only) had a richly plastered ceiling, this time in a free mix of French Baroque and Indian styles. Floors and walls were clad in pink, brown and white polished marble. The auditorium showed Matcham at his best as he fully realised the possibilities of using his patented cantilevers to develop a vibrant three-dimensional arrangement. Boxes and balconies occurred in every possible plane, sweeping round, bending and bulging in and out to optimise the sight-lines and disappearing into mysterious niches, painted with murals and filled with statuary.

Above: An artist's impression of the interior of Hengler's Circus amphitheatre. (Bruce Peter collection)

Left: The Empire Theatre, Sauchiehall Street, Glasgow (Frank Matcham, 1897) – home to variety and also cinema shows. (Tony Moss collection, CTA Archive)

Below: Trongate in Glasgow in the 1920s with the Panopticon cinema (formerly the Britannia Music Hall) on the right-hand side. (Bruce Peter collection)

The Empire was determinedly respectable and it became one of the most successful variety venues in the city, winning a popularity which would not diminish until its final closure and ultimate demolition in 1963. (It had by that time also won a rather different notoriety in the mythology of music hall as the 'graveyard of English comics'.) As early as 5 May 1897, within its first month of operation, *The Bailie,* Glasgow's premier listings journal and magazine, advertised the Lumière Cinematographe as part of the bill at the Empire:

'The original Lumière Cinematograph, From the Empire Palace, London.
Lumiere's Cinematograph … in an entirely new series of pictures.'

On 2 June 1897, the Empire again featured film on its programme and on this occasion it was not a Lumière projector but a Biograph which was in use "To-night and during the Week. Invented by Herman Casler of New York. The Biograph… The latest American sensation in animated photographs." (*The Bailie*, 2 June 1897.) The event is also described in more detail in the 'Monday Gossip' feature of the same edition of *The Bailie*:

'Quite a 'monstre' – 'monstre,' not monster – company is appearing this week at the Empire. The leading feature in the nightly programme is supplied by 'The American Biograph', the latest sensation in animated photography. All the figures thrown upon the screen by the Biograph are of life size, and consequently the scenes in which they take part have a wonderful sense of reality. Among them are the rush of New York fire engines to the scene of a conflagration, the whirring of express trains in and out of a station, and the boiling, seething, Niagara Rapids. Various humorous groups are also represented… these include a pillow fight among children, a boy chasing a kitten, and a negress playing with her little piccaninny. Among the general members of the Empire company are the Sisters Preston, [and] George Lashwood….'

The engagement of the Biograph was clearly popular as it was retained for the next week's programme. The Empire's own advertisement (in *The Bailie*, 9 June 1897) is keen to indicate this success:

'The Directors have pleasure in announcing that at very considerable expense they have been successful in retaining the Biograph for one week longer. 'The Biograph' is without doubt the most Successful Exhibition of Animated Photographs ever witnessed in Glasgow.'

By the end of the year, the regular appearance of film in the listings suggests that its value as part of an evening's variety bill had been proven. Film had featured at not only the Empire, but also at Arthur Hubner's Britannia, a considerably less salubrious music hall located on Glasgow's Trongate. The Britannia had started life in 1857 as Campbell's Music Saloon, an unlicensed music hall owned by a Mr Brand and run by an actor called Willie Campbell. The entrance was only a few doors wide, and was sandwiched between shop fronts. Looking along the street, it was marked only by two gas lanterns. There was a small hallway with ticket booths on either side. The auditorium was on the first and second floors and had a single wooden balcony on iron columns with bench seating throughout (this structure had been rescued from an abandoned church prior to demolition). Hubner moved his cinema shows there from the Ice Skating Palace. Prices ranged from 3d in the pit to 6d in the cushioned forms of the circle. The *Glasgow Weekly Programme* informed readers that 'To those who like music-hall business, the BEST and CHEAPEST is undoubtedly the BRITANNIA in Trongate'.

At the same time, a remarkable a new attraction – E. H. Bostock's **Scottish Zoo and Grand Variety Circus** – opened in New City Road, Cowcaddens on the other side of central Glasgow. Bostock was born into a famous circus family from Buckinghamshire. Apart from menageries in Portobello and Glasgow, his family's firm, Bostock & Wombwell, also ran several theatres, circuses and cinemas in East Anglia. Bostock's Glasgow project was a huge warehouse-like iron-framed structure which not only housed a circus arena and stables for everything from horses to elephants, but also a roller skating rink and a number of side-shows. It was a veritable indoor entertainment palace. Opened on 2 May 1897, it was designed by Bertie Crewe – a leading London-based theatre architect who specialised in producing opulent and technically-sophisticated variety houses – and partly financed by Thomas Barrasford, a Newcastle-based variety impresario. In his 1927 autobiography *Menageries,*

Circuses and Theatres, Bostock described his early use of film as a 'side-show' feature of the entertainments on offer at the zoo for which he charged a penny admission. He notes that in the winter of 1897-98 he 'exhibited a pantomime film (beautifully coloured by hand by a Paris firm), which was seen on both sides of the circus and which proved a great attraction'. This suggests that the screen was hung above the ring and, consequently, that half the audience saw a back-projected reversed image.

Also in 1897, the circus proprietor Albert Hengler opened a rival to Bostock's Scottish Zoo and Grand Variety Circus. **Hengler's Circus Hippodrome** was prominently located only a short stroll away in the former Ice Skating Palace at 326 Sauchiehall Street in central Glasgow. The two similar attractions were now in head-to-head competition. Hengler's opening programme declared:

> 'The provision of a place of entertainment that in its equipment and elegance of design shall be worthy of the Second City of the Empire has been the object aimed at by the proprietors of the Hippodrome…The great steel roof trusses have been covered up with a dome-shaped ceiling of fibre plaster decorated in rich colours, having large cartouche-like panels with spirited drawings of horses and riders in Roman chariots that seem to leap from the clouds, while the old bare brick walls are now clothed in a rich golden covering.
> Once inside, the amphitheatre has seating for over 1500….and the ring in front of the proscenium is 142 feet in circumference… by an elaborate mechanical contrivance (this) can be converted within one minute into a huge lake of water… The architect from whose plans the building has been constructed is Mr James Miller of Blythswood Square, who was the architect for the Glasgow International Exhibition in 1901, the most successful exhibition of modern times.'

Miller was ideally suited to the job. His exhibition pavilions had been remarkably theatrical with great domes and Indian motifs, but he was also technically very proficient, designing everything from churches and banks to Glasgow Subway stations.

Between the long circus seasons, Hengler now found profitable use in running his own premises as a cinema. Rows of seats were fitted over the arena so that an audience of more than 2,000 could watch. An article in *Milden Miscellany* recalled:

> '…Several flights of steps divided by brass and iron handrails led up to the entrance hall which was painted bright red. The stone corridors had a peculiar smell, not unlike that of a tenement close after it had been washed and pipe-clayed. But there was also an essence of something essentially Hengler's. In the off-seasons, children trooped to Hengler's from all parts of Glasgow on Saturday afternoons to pay their penny admission and climb up to the gallery, where wandering eyes paused momentarily at the site of voluptuous ladies reclining against gilded cornucopias on the frescoed heights. The screen was on a wooden frame and could be lowered and raised like a kitchen pulley….'

Remarkably, although both Bostock's and Hengler's premises closed shortly after the First World War (in 1918 and 1924 respectively), their remnants can still be identified today. The structure of the Scottish Zoo and Variety Circus is now hidden behind later façades and houses a snooker club and Glasgow's Chinatown. After an unsuccessful spell as a ballroom, Hengler's Circus was radically re-built as the Regal Cinema (later the ABC – see below). Passers-by climbing Scott Street can still see brick fragments from the old circus in the cinema's side wall while, inside, the remains of animal pens were discovered below the auditorium when the building was converted to a multiplex in the latter-1970s. Presently, it serves as a live music venue, named the O2 ABC.

The Travelling Cinema

THE entrepreneurial acumen of the showmen was quickly aroused by the possibilities of film as instanced by the Greens, Kemps and Codonas. Like the Moss family, the Greens and several other of the most famous early cinema-owning families began as showmen or carnival operators whose show-booths attended the seasonal fairs throughout the land. The Greens were a large family of Lancashire showmen, a branch of which moved from their native Wigan to Glasgow in search of better fortunes. George Green, the head of the family, was quick to see potential in the fledgling cinema. He was in London in the autumn of 1896, looking for a new novelty for the Carnival at Vinegar Hill in Glasgow, when he visited the Empire Theatre, Leicester Square, and met Robert Paul, regarded as the founder of the British film industry. His invention, the Animatograph, was just what Green was looking for, and so he negotiated the purchase of one of Paul's projectors to take back to Scotland. Following experiments in the cellar of the Farmer's Arms in Preston, its first use was in the Circus building at the Carnival in Glasgow.

Glasgow Cross was the traditional centre of entertainments in the city – its earliest music halls were all to be found huddled in streets close to the Tollbooth in the Saltmarket, just a stone's throw away from both Glasgow Green and Vinegar Hill, the celebrated sites of the annual fair where entertainments of every description could be found. Theatricals of all descriptions, including early film screenings, were staged in 'geggies' – the Scottish manifestation of the booth or fit-up theatre. The traditional aspect of Green's involvement with the fairs is indicated by another listings magazine, the *Glasgow Weekly Programme* (16 July 1906):

'A sure sign of the approach of the Glasgow Fair is the bustling activity at the Vinegar Hill Carnival, the mecca during the holidays of thousands of the city's workers who are spending their vacation and money in the town. For months the showground is deserted, but at the Fair and New Year the caravans return, stalls and shows are erected, and for a week or so the ancient Gallowgate is crowded with young people en route for the Carnival, or else returning over-laden with 'prizes.' This year arrangements are being made to cope with huge crowds, when the usual attractions in the way of hobby-horses, the switchback railway, ghost illusions and dolly shows will be supplemented by motor car roundabouts and a variety entertainment. The carnival is an institution inseparably associated with Glasgow holidays [and] is the accepted sign of prowess there. Mr. Green works hard for the people in the way of entertainments, and richly deserves his well-earned success.'

During the 1898 season Green introduced a novel fairground booth, known as **Green's Cinematograph**. Consecutive reconstructions of this booth clearly illustrate the affinity of early cinema architecture with showmanship. Initially, it was 50ft by 30ft inside, offering standing room only for about 500 jam-packed patrons. The images shown in the booth were considered so lifelike that, according to one account, possibly apocryphal, when pictures of Fingal's Cave were screened, a number of visitors vacated the booth concerned that they would be drenched by the oncoming tide dashing against the rocks!

Yet, even then a distinct attitude to cinema architecture had developed – typically consisting of an

23

Top left: Green's fairground with the Whitevale Theatre in the background. (Bruce Peter collection)

Top right: Green's Cinematograph booth. (Tommy Green collection)

Above: Glasgow's Gallowgate in the 1900s with the splendid wooden entrance to the fairground, the perimeter walls of which are generously adorned with advertisements. The aesthetic of the fair influenced cinema architecture as it developed in the ensuing years. (Bruce Peter collection)

Below left: A subsequent enlarged Green's cinema booth. (Tommy Green collection)

Below right: Green's final cinema booth, with towers added looking rather like an early permanent cinema. (Tommy Green collection)

ornate neo-baroque façade, illuminated by hundreds of incandescent bulbs, complemented with jaunty music from a steam organ. Green's Cinematograph show was later modified with the addition of a Gavioli organ built into the show-front, with steps up to the show and a front stage for the paraders – gaily-costumed showmen who heralded the delights within. They were essential at fairs where show-booths were in intense competition to attract custom from their rivals. The remainder of Green's Cinematograph was a rudimentary canvas tent containing cramped rows of wooden benches. The booth travelled both in Scotland and south of the border from fair to fair by rail, and its success no doubt encouraged Green to devise even more elaborate improvements. The show-front was extended and new carved decoration was added around the enlarged side-entrances and above the organ. When towers were placed at either end, it took on the appearance of a permanent cinema. These improvements to the frontage were intended to make the booth resemble fairground booths seen by Harry Bradley, formerly employed by George Green as a manager, at Luna Park on Coney Island in New York. Bradley soon returned to re-join Green's operation and he eventually built his own cinema, the **Picture House** in Kirkconnel in Ayrshire. Green's Cinematograph was now 52ft in length but even more painted and carved panels were added to the front, making it among the most elaborate of travelling cinema booths ever seen.

Next, Green decided to acquire a permanent hall. In 1908 he bought the **Whitevale Theatre,** a 1000 seat music hall in the Gallowgate. The land around the new cinema was used as a park for showmen's caravans and Mrs Green collected a shilling a week for each stance. The family moved into a flat above the Whitevale's pay box and they were all soon involved in running the cinema. Building on the success of the Whitevale, George Green opened a chain of '**Picturedromes**' around Glasgow, starting in the Gorbals in March 1911. The Picturedromes, typically, had twin towered façades, similar in appearance to Green's earlier Cinematograph show-booth. George Green died in November 1915 but under his sons, Fred and Bert, the cinema business continued to expand.

Another venturer was George Kemp who trained initially as a solicitor's clerk in Leicester but, no doubt yearning for a more adventurous life, he became a travelling showman instead (at first he advertised himself

as 'The Midget King'). Initially, he toured novelty and freak shows. In 1901, by which time his freak show was reputedly the biggest in England, he purchased a new two-wagon Cinematograph show. The front was decorated with elaborate gilded carving, and was further adorned with electric lights. "Mr. Kemp should know whether elaborate fronts are worth the investment," reported *The Showman,* "for he has travelled with his novelties throughout the whole of America as well as the British Isles." It was an excellent time to launch the show as films of the Boer War were particularly popular, and Kemp claimed to be the first to show images of this conflict. He now promoted himself as 'President' Kemp, probably a reference to his visits to the United States. A 1909 report in *The Showman* recorded that Kemp was 'Resplendent in his grey frock coat suit, as he stood on the front stage, side by side with a noble Redman in all the glory of war paint [and] an Eskimo in silver furs, with a real live teddy bear for all to see.' Amongst the films screened was one of Shackleton at the South Pole, whilst another was 'England Invaded' in honour of which he had the exterior of his show decorated with the national colours. During 1910, near record business was created when films of Edward VII's funeral were screened. Shortly afterwards, Kemp also took the decision to build a permanent cinema, and so in 1911 his purpose-built **Pavilion** was opened in Johnstone. As with Green's Whitevale, the 1000 seat Pavilion also included a flat for Kemp's family, but the involvement in permanent picture-houses meant that the travelling show played a less important role in his business and it was put into storage.

On 6 October 1913 George Kemp and his son, Harry, opened their third new cinema, the luxurious 900 seat **La Scala** in Saltcoats, a Clyde coastal resort where they already operated the primitive **Casino** cinema. He then advertised his travelling cinematograph show for sale in *World Fair* magazine between June and August 1913. It was described as 'admittedly the best … it strikes consternation to the heart of each picture hall manager in every town it visits.' The truth was quite the reverse as permanent cinemas were actually taking a great deal of business away from the travelling shows. Nonetheless, George Green bought the show in September 1913. The Greens and the Kemps had a close relationship as George Kemp's son, Harry, was married to Green's niece. The Greens advertised for staff for the show and it was,

  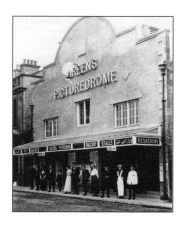

Top left: Harry Bradley's Picture House in Kirkconnel in the 1920s.
(Tommy Green collection)

Top middle: Green's Picturedrome in Ballater Street, Gorbals (Thomas Baird Jr, 1911) photographed prior to demolition in the 1960s.
(Tony Moss collection, CTA Archive)

Top right: Green's Picturedrome, Irvine (John Fairweather, 1912).
(Tony Moss collection, CTA Archive)

Centre: Houstoun Square in Johnstone in the early 1920s showing George Kemp's Pavilion cinema on the right-hand side. Note also the bandstand and the recently erected war memorial. (Bruce Peter collection)

Left: Green's Picturedrome in Wellshot Road, Tollcross, Glasgow (John Fairweather, 1914) nestles amongst the tenements. (Bruce Peter collection)

ironically, Walter Kemp, George Kemp's brother, who had previously managed **Green's Picturedrome** in Ayr, who was selected to handle the business. By the end of the 1914 season George Green offered for sale all the equipment concerned with the travelling side of his business as he too decided to concentrate on developing permanent cinemas. Later, in 1919, Kemp sold the Pavilion at Johnstone to George Green Ltd to finance further cinema expansion in Saltcoats, while Green's concentrated their activities in and around Glasgow. By then semi-retired, George Kemp continued to assist in the business until his death in 1928. His son, Harry, worked hard and expanded the chain, which in post-war years included four cinemas plus substantial property and commercial interests.

William Codona was born in 1862 into a show family in the Scottish mining village of Waterloo near Wishaw in Lanarkshire. Codona began work on Scott's Circus, where he met his first wife, Mary Anne Kennedy. Together they travelled with a portable Bioscope show and variety theatre. A 1914 advertisement for The

Bioscope requested 'actors for Codona's Magnet Theatre, also scenery painter and a man who can run through about 1,000 foot of pictures nightly.' Codona also operated the Bioscope in local halls around Edinburgh. By the advent of the First World War, the showmen had set up mostly permanent cinemas. (Codona's travelling cinema booth was converted to a permanent venue in 1914, located in Haddington, but by 1919 he had opened a purpose-built cinema at Tranent.)

Much of the carnival razzmatazz, however, clung to the cinema as its status developed and it moved from fairground to city to suburb: a vividly uniformed staff, parties, ceremonies, music and brilliant night-time illumination were part of the allure. Meanwhile, in the densely-populated and industrial Central Belt of Scotland other entrepreneurs bought cinema equipment to tour with their own travelling cinema shows by hiring any available public hall. Among these were Bennell, Singleton, Pringle, Maxwell and Scott.

James Joseph Bennell first came to the attention of Scottish audiences as the manager of Sydney Carter's

Above left: George Kemp's Casino cinema in Hamilton Street, Saltcoats (1910). (Richard Stenlake collection)

Above right: Kemp's subsequent La Scala, opposite the Casino. (Bruce Peter collection)

Below left: 'Kemp's Scotch Broth Entertainers' at La Scala in the 1920s: variety was an extra summer attraction at the popular seaside resort town. (Bruce Peter collection)

Below right: Codona's Cinema in Haddington perhaps converted from a travelling cinematograph booth. (Bruce Peter collection)

Pictures, a travelling show which visited Aberdeen, Edinburgh and Glasgow in 1906. The Glasgow performances took place in the august setting of the St Andrew's Halls and were so successful that Andrew Freer, the Halls' manager, advised Bennell to find a permanent venue in the city, which he soon did. Bennell's first cinema had an odd background. The temperance movement had long been active in Glasgow, one of their activities being to organise non-alcoholic entertainments including Saturday evening tea concerts in Good Templars' Harmonic Association halls. These harmless amusements were fondly known as 'The Bursts' (everyone in the audience was given an orange and an apple in a paper bag and at a set time all the empty 'pokes' were blown up and burst simultaneously to great cheering and clapping). By the end of the first decade of the century their appeal was waning and they were eventually abandoned, leaving many Good Templars' halls unused.

Bennell chose the largest of them, the **Wellington Palace,** in Commercial Road, Gorbals, which, like so many early cinemas, had started life as a music hall. He squeezed a projection room into the rear stalls, leaving

J.J. Bennell, who believed that the cinema improved the quality of peoples' lives, particularly in densely-populated working class districts. (Scottish Screen Archive)

room for an audience of nearly 2,000 adults. 'Bennell's Brilliants' made a slow start in November 1909 but picked up enormously after an extensive promotional campaign in which whole streets at a time were circulated with smartly produced leaflets. The programme for each week was headed patriotically with the name of a British battleship and the stories of the silent films were outlined enticingly. To boost business families were offered two free passes entitling the bearers to admission if they bought a penny programme.

To Gorbals children, Bennell's BB (Bright and Beautiful) Pictures quickly became an institution and during the Wellington Palace's first months the children probably had as much effect as the leafleting in promoting the shows. Up to 3,000 children could be squeezed onto benches to enjoy films at the Saturday afternoon 'BBs.' Bennell's ebullient personality appealed to them. He was like a friendly uncle who greeted them at the pay box with a smile and a pat on the head and then stood in front of the screen to teach them the BB song:

'The BB Pictures they're all right,
Ever beautiful and bright,
We will sing with all our might
Go and see them every night!'

The jingle could be heard all over the Gorbals. Bennell had an interesting programming philosophy, which no doubt contributed to his success. The pictures shown in the evenings were the same as those shown at the children's matinées; he believed that if a film was not good enough for children it was not good enough for their parents.

Simultaneously, Bennell hired the **Albert Hall** in Shandwick Place, Edinburgh. It had been built in 1876 as a venue for 'improving' lectures called The Albert Institute of Fine Arts. By 1880, this had failed and it was re-opened as a music hall. By 1886, however, it had become a Methodist Mission, before turning into a cinema. On 1 February 1910, the *Evening News* heralded a grand re-opening with Tindle's Picture Concerts – a cine-variety show mixing music hall acts with films and orchestral accompaniment. (Tindle was brother-in-law of Richard Thornton, then partner in the Moss Empires theatre chain.) By 1915 it had become a full-time cinema once more, and although closed in 1932 the ornate entrance portico can still be seen today.

In Dundee, Bennell's BB Pictures became popular at the **Oxford Hall** in Logie Street. Dating from 1912, it was a rather basic venue with only a single raked floor and upholstered benches in the front stalls; it nestled among the Logie Street tenements in the city's Lochee district. Bennell leased the hall from its owner and manager, Arthur Binnall, a local entrepreneur, who supervised its day-to-day running. This arrangement benefited both parties and gave Bennell a useful Scottish foothold in the film distribution business by supplying others. This was an arm of the cinema industry which was growing in importance. Binnall too found prosperity as he went on to develop his own cinema circuit around Dundee. In the 1920s, the Oxford Hall became known as the **West End Cinema** and later, when sold to the Gray circuit in the 1930s, it became the grandly-titled **Astoria**. It was later demolished and replaced by flats. (Incidentally, Dundee's largest and most respectable

temporary cinema venue in the early days of the medium was the **Caird Hall** which had the biggest screen in the city, stretched across the organ gallery, and reputedly the longest projection throw in the whole of Britain.)

In 1908 Richard Vincent Singleton began his travelling cinema show. As a founding member of the Labour Party and a supporter of the Suffragette Movement, he was a staunch Socialist who believed in the self-improvement of the working classes. His son, George, was born in a tenement in Glasgow's Bridgeton district. Singleton had originally been in the printing business but he was quick to realise the possibilities which cinema offered. His first shows were given in public halls around Lanarkshire and Clydeside. George Singleton recalled that:

'We would move in and tie up a screen against one wall. The films may have been silent, but nothing else

The ornate entrance to the Albert Hall in Edinburgh's Shandwick Place, photographed in the 1970s. This was home to Bennell's BB Pictures in Edinburgh.
(Tony Moss collection, CTA Archive)

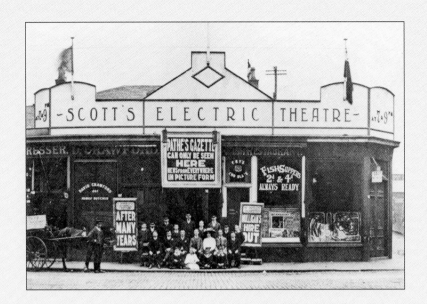

Top left: Scott's Electric Theatre in Glasgow's Gallowgate (1909).
(Tony Moss collection, CTA Archive)

Top right: George Urie Scott, pictured here later in life, was one of Glasgow's great entertainment impresarios.
(Scottish Screen Archive)

Centre: The Paragon in Glasgow's Gorbals was obviously converted from a church, as this 1930s image shows. (Bruce Peter collection)

Right: Another image of the Paragon, this time dating from the 1950s and probably taken shortly before the building was demolished. (Bruce Peter collection)

was. The projector was set up in the middle of the audience and it rattled and clanked relentlessly. Those highly flammable nitrate film spools would be lying around on the floor and our customers would just drop their cigarette ends and tap out their pipes among them. It terrifies me to think about it now, but there were few safety regulations in the old days. All the while, I walked around with a tray shouting, 'caramels, chocolates, toffee!' As the film started we'd all be plunged into darkness, there were no dimmers in those days, and my father, who loved music, would be thumping away on the piano at the side. Babies would cry, conversations would continue and those who could read would repeat the captions in loud voices for the benefit of the illiterate and short-sighted around them. When a spool broke, everyone would hiss and stamp their feet.'

Ralph Pringle, meanwhile, was touring his 'North American Animated Cinematograph' around leased halls throughout Scotland and the North of England. By 1909 Pringle owned a chain of cinemas. In Edinburgh he ran the **Picture Palace** in Grove Street and **Pringle's New Picture Palace** (later the **Garrick**) which had opened at 41 Elm Row on 16 November 1908. In Glasgow Pringle rented the Queen's Theatre, a music hall occupying the upper floors of a block in Watson Street, just east of Glasgow Cross, which he re-launched as **Pringle's Picture Palace** in November 1907, and shortly afterwards he converted the Alexander Assembly Halls in Cowcaddens into the **Bijou Picture Palace**, subsequently known to its patrons as 'The By Jove.'

Scotland's most successful cinema entrepreneur, John Maxwell, began his cinema career as partner and legal adviser to a company which hired Pollokshaws Burgh Hall for film shows. Born in 1876, Maxwell was a small, unassuming, canny Scotsman who had been a family solicitor in Glasgow, but evidently knew a lucrative investment when he saw one. He was also reputedly a shrewd and cultured man, widely read and quick-witted. In Glasgow, his legal expertise won him esteem; his partnership in the law firm Maxwell, Hodgson & Company gave him an authority in the city's cinema industry, which was then dominated by itinerant showmen, that was unequalled. He was also interested in politics and had stood unsuccessfully as the Liberal candidate in Motherwell in the 1922

Election (incidentally, he was beaten by the Communist candidate).

In 1912, Maxwell was offered shares in the first **Princes** cinema in Glasgow's Springburn district and soon he acquired an interest in a dozen other cinemas and theatres across Central Scotland by purchasing much of the R.C. Buchanan chain (see below). In 1917 he founded Scottish Cinema and Variety Theatres with its head office in Glasgow. In 1924, Maxwell formed Savoy Cinemas with an office in London. This firm acquired many second-hand cinemas throughout England. Maxwell's business interests continued to expand through the purchase both of individual cinemas and entire circuits and his various subsidiaries were eventually merged as Associated British Cinemas in 1928. In addition to his ABC empire, Maxwell controlled British International Pictures, which made *Blackmail* (the first talking picture made in Britain, directed by the young Alfred Hitchcock), and owned Waverley Films, Scotland's largest distributor. Controlling distribution as well as exhibition was a boon to Maxwell's business. Since around 1912, film renters had largely been able to dictate the terms of film exhibition, but not to John Maxwell.

In Scotland's larger towns and cities, new purpose-built cinemas quickly superseded travelling cinema shows. In Lanarkshire, however, the Paulos, a fairground family, continued to give cinema performances in halls in the smaller mining villages, touring these on a weekly rotation and giving performances for one night only in each. This continued until the 1950s. In the Highlands, on the other hand, travelling cinema shows became the norm for smaller communities and many village halls were converted for the purpose with their own projection booths, some of which can still be seen today.

With film so popular it was inevitable that film exhibition should develop apace from primitive travelling shows, setting up wherever they could find a suitable space, to relatively comfortable, efficient venues, many of which were notable examples of a prolific and fascinating architectural genre. This trend was accelerated by the Kinematograph Act, which arose out of government and public concern about the fire risk posed by the highly volatile nitrate-based celluloid film, especially when passing through projectors with naked carbon arc flames.

The first generation of properly planned conversions and purpose-built cinemas emerged to take account of

Top left: The New Bedford (1921) was another converted church, this time with a façade in the neo-classical manner, designed by J. Jeffrey Waddell. (Glasgow City Archives)

Top right: The BB Cinerama in Perth (1913), yet another converted church, but this one substantially re-built to the extent that its origins are concealed. (Bruce Peter collection)

Centre: The auditorium of the Perth BB Cinerama, a typical provincial cinema of the early twentieth century with a barrel-vaulted ceiling and an almost square proscenium opening. (Bruce Peter collection)

Below left: Green's Picturedrome in Ayr (James Campbell Reid, 1910) was converted from a roller skating rink and had an ornate show façade fronting a corrugated metal shed. (Bruce Peter collection)

Below right: The Picture House in Constitution Street, Leith, converted from a Turkish Baths, today remains an intact example of an early cinema. The fact that it has been converted to a church perhaps shows how interchangeable the two genres are. (Bruce Peter)

the new regulations. Soon after the Act was passed, in Glasgow alone there were more than fifty licensed halls in operation (this includes public halls licensed for occasional film shows) and the city's first purpose-built cinema, the **Charing Cross Electric Theatre,** opened in Sauchiehall Street on 12 May 1910. This was designed by George A. Boswell and inserted into the ground and first floors of an existing red sandstone-faced commercial block by Robert Duncan, dating from 1898. Boswell, born in 1879 and practicing in Glasgow, became an early and prolific architect of such cinemas, often simply converted from shop units. Moreover, the shift into proper cinemas signalled that film was becoming respectable. The pattern was similar in Edinburgh and Aberdeen, yet most venues continued to offer a mixed bill of film and variety acts. In Edinburgh, meanwhile, venues advertising films exclusively included the **Operetta House** in Chambers Street (a former music hall which had begun showing Edison's Animated Pictures in 1900) and the **North British Electric Theatre**, opened in 1903 (later the **Cinema House**) in Nicholson Street. Each of these was fashioned from pre-existing music hall premises. From then on competition for the growing and increasingly enthusiastic cinema-going public was fierce and it was to spawn a remarkable number and diversity of cinemas in coming decades.

For entertainment entrepreneurs in industrial areas, having a cinematograph licence soon proved a warrant to make money. As cinema grew rapidly in popularity, any remotely suitable hall was adapted and many existing entertainment premises were hurriedly converted to picture halls. Many of the first cinemas were simply re-vamped from shop units – such as the **Electric Theatre** in Dundee's Nethergate (1910) – Dundee's first full-time cinema. It was run by local businessmen and the projectionist, Mr Peter Feathers, was a Dundee optician and an early cinematography enthusiast. Films were shown between 2.30 pm and 10.30 pm and the price of admission included a cup of tea and a biscuit. The small frontage of the Electric was typical of such early cinemas, being ornately decorated, brightly painted and illuminated by countless electric light bulbs to lure passers-by to come inside.

Scott's Electric Theatre opened in 1909 in the former Annfield Halls on Glasgow's Gallowgate, located not far from Green's Whitevale. This primitive cinema was significant as it was the first to be designed by Charles

J. McNair, who later became one of Scotland's most prolific cinema designers (see below). Its owner was George Urie Scott, an entrepreneur who was to become one of the leading figures in the Scottish cinema industry, as a financier, developer and owner. Born in Glasgow in 1882, Scott began his career apprenticed to a cabinet maker. A small man with red hair and a ruddy complexion, his unassuming manner belied great ambition and energy. He became involved in variety theatres and, before long, had interests in the entertainment business ranging from ballroom dancing (he owned the Dennistoun Palais) to variety (he also owned the Empress and Pavilion Theatres, where he nurtured native talents such as Jack Anthony and Lex McLean). In 1908 he formed Scott's Electric Theatres and the company was soon running seven primitive picture houses in Glasgow, Lanarkshire and the Borders. By the thirties Scott had launched the Cinema Construction Company, a joint venture with McNair. Before the Second World War they built almost all of what were to become the ABC cinemas in Scotland as well as a number of super cinemas for independent operators (see below).

In Glasgow's densely-populated Gorbals area, where grim tenements consisting of 'single ends' (one-room dwellings) and 'room and kitchens' were mixed with small industrial premises, a number of ingenious conversions took place. When the Free and United Presbyterian Churches merged in 1901 to form the United Free Church, a glut of superfluous church buildings became available. Although these were usually spartan and often had poor sight-lines to the cinema screen (due to their balcony slips being supported on columns and some pews being at right angles to the front) a number were converted.

In 1912, a Gorbals bookie known as Wee Titch (nicknamed after a popular music hall star called Little Titch) converted a Free Church building in Cumberland Street into the **Paragon**. Wee Titch intended to operate it himself and had installed a manager called George Archibald, but he sold it instead to Richard V. Singleton who was keen to get part of the lucrative Gorbals cinema business. Richard's son George recalled that Archibald 'left soon after father bought the place. He became the manager of the **New Bedford** (see below), went on to become the managing director of Odeon Cinemas and subsequently supervised United Artists' activities in

Above: Another view of the interior of the former Picture House in Leith, showing old tip-up cinema seats and part of the decoration on the front of the small balcony. (Bruce Peter)
Below: The Oxford Playhouse cinema (Lennox & McMath, 1921) was converted from an old tramway depot for Bernard Frutin's circuit. (Tony Moss collection, CTA Archive)

Britain when they took a stake in Odeon in 1940. He ended up as Lord Archibald, a far cry from his early days at the Paragon in the old Gorbals'. Apart from new external canopies and a projection room, the building was hardly altered from its original use and the dingy interior even retained the church pews. George Singleton remembered that 'the patrons were a tough and dirty lot and to maintain cleanliness the place was 'saturated in carbolic disinfectant', but that the Paragon was 'a good earner as father and I would fill every last pew'.

In nearby Laurieston, Wee Titch next converted a former United Presbyterian Church with an austere, neo-classical frontage into the New Bedford cinema. Opened in 1921, it too was quickly sold on to another up-and-coming Glasgow cinema entrepreneur – Bernard Frutin, the owner of the city's Metropole Music Hall. Elsewhere, The **Grove** in Breadalbane Street was a conversion of the Sandyford United Free Church, and was opened in 1915. The Kent Road West United Free Church became the **New Kent** cinema in 1921. The Grove and the New Kent, like so many other smaller

picture-houses, good and bad, foundered in the face of competition from the new generation of super cinemas. All except the Paragon were closed by the early 1930s.

In Perth, J. J. Bennell purchased an abandoned United Free church in Victoria Street and had it converted to the **BB Cinerama**. This was later enlarged with the addition of a balcony, and so the side walls were simply heightened with brick and a new roof was added. Remarkably, this austere building continued until 1962 and remained in existence until recently as a bingo club. Still extant is a former church in Coldstream, near the border, which became the **Eildon Cinema** and is now a community centre, with a decaying neon cinema sign still attached to the steeple.

A number of cinemas were also converted from roller skating rinks (in the 1890s, there was a craze for roller skating which led to the construction of many rinks). Back in Glasgow, the early success of his Wellington Palace in the Gorbals led J. J. Bennell to lease the Victoria Road Roller Skating Rink, a massive corrugated iron shed

behind a neo-classical façade close to Eglinton Toll, and convert it into another **BB Cinerama.** When opened in September 1912 *The Glasgow Herald* praised its appointments: 'A prettily decorated vestibule with tea-rooms on either side gives access to the auditorium, also very effectively designed. Seating accommodation is provided for about 1,500 people and, in respect of heating and ventilation, everything has been done for the comfort of visitors.' This was a cause for congratulation since conversions of this kind were notoriously uncomfortable. The first Cinerama was such a success that Bennell opened a new purpose-built one, only a few hundred metres away, in October 1922.

In Ayr George Green Ltd purchased the failing Ayr Roller Rink at Boswell Park and re-built it as Green's Picturedrome cinema, opening in June 1911. Behind an ornate frontage, it made a very rudimentary cinema, and so it was closed in 1922 for a massive reconstruction. It emerged as **Green's Playhouse**, seating about 2,000. The **Olympia** in Murray Place, Stirling, was a much

The Standard Picture House in Glasgow's Dumbarton Road was a very rudimentary structure in the back court of a tenement, as this 1930s image shows. (Tony Moss collection, CTA Archive)

smaller roller skating hall which became a picture-house in 1911. It burned down in a spectacular fire ten years later.

Among the varied premises that became cinemas, few were more exotic than the **Picture House** in Constitution Street, Leith, which was converted from a Turkish baths in 1913 (this explains its peculiar façade, capped with small minarets). Astonishingly, it survives today as a Christian centre and in largely intact condition. Its side walls have simple plaster ornamentation and there is a single shallow balcony to the rear. Most interesting, however, are its rows of hard tip-up seats with spindly cast iron frames and hard leather cushions and backs in thick wooden frames – a survival from its early days.

Some other early conversions were also remarkable. The **Oxford Playhouse** cinema in Glasgow's industrial Springburn district was converted from a tram depot, while the **Ardgowan** in the city's Tradeston area was fashioned out of a defunct cork factory. Consequently, it was nicknamed 'The Corkie' by the locals. Wooden benches accommodated an audience of 1,116 and the cavernous but dingy interior with exposed roof trusses was illuminated by gas. Mrs Jean Melvin remembers the hall full of children eating oranges, a nutritious gift from its management, and spitting the pips at each other. The smallest children were singled out as targets and had to take refuge under the benches. The Ardgowan survived until 1963. Today, it is long-gone and even the street pattern of Tradeston has changed out of all recognition through subsequent slum clearance and comprehensive redevelopment schemes.

Similarly grim was the **Standard Picture House** on Dumbarton Road. Opened in 1910 as the **Alexandra Hall**, it was hidden in a back court at 95 Dumbarton Road. Its nickname, the 'Palais de Scratch', indicates its quality and was a reference to Fyfe & Fyfe's luxurious Palais de Danse in the next block. Duncan Cree remembers matinée performances at the Standard in the early thirties:

'We were jammed onto long wooden benches at the front of the hall. There was loud cheering when the lights dimmed for a singsong led by the lady pianist. The words were projected onto the screen:
    Don't throw stones at your mother,
    She'll wash you and put you to bed.
    Don't throw stones at your mother,
    Throw bricks at your father instead!'

The Standard was one of a number of cinemas built in the back greens of tenements. Picture-houses in these locations not only robbed the occupants of the surrounding tenements of their drying and playing areas but also blocked out daylight and prevented fresh air from entering into their homes. Nevertheless, permission was usually granted for their construction by local authorities as cinemas offered cheap local entertainment for poorer citizens and provided a warm sheltered place away from the cramped conditions of many homes. They kept some out of pubs and others out of trouble. Perhaps these considerations were felt to outweigh any possible nuisance factors for their neighbours.

From Theatre to Cinema

LOOKING back on 'Glasgow Amusements During the Year' of 1911 the *Glasgow Programme and Exhibition Journal* (11 December) comments on the rise of cinemas in Glasgow:

'Perhaps the next most eventful thing [after the 1911 Scottish Exhibition of Natural History, Art and Industry held in Glasgow] in connection with our city, has been the rapid rise in the popularity of the Picture Houses; it is said that there are close on one hundred of these places open every evening in the city of Glasgow and suburbs, and they are not all so well conducted as those in Sauchiehall Street, but on the whole there is no doubt they are exercising an educative effect on the mass of the people. Also on the other hand they are reducing the attendances very much at our better class Theatres and Halls.'

It must be remembered that, unlike today when theatres are widely subsidised, in the Edwardian period they were commercial entertainments and their owners were determined to maximise profits wherever possible. For theatres particularly in suburban and provincial locations, going over to the enemy – cinema – became irresistible. This saved greatly on booking touring companies for seasons of drama, opera or variety.

During the Edwardian era, a final generation of theatres was developed in the densely-populated suburbs of Glasgow in particular. In order to attract 'upmarket' audiences and to justify the higher admission prices compared to those of the rival picture-houses, these theatres had to offer a superior level of comfort to all of their patrons. Thus, they were 'bigger boned' than their Victorian counterparts. No doubt attempting to emulate

the success of Moss' Empire, these suburban theatres were all fitted with projection booths and had cinema screens on frames which could be retracted into their fly towers when the stage was in use. They were, in effect, multi-purpose auditoria which could be programmed equally for operetta, drama, pantomime, variety, cinema shows and even lectures with accompanying lantern slides. Consequently, they were designed with balconies facing the stage rather more squarely than the earlier generation to give a more direct view of the flat cinema screen from the majority of seats. This aspect of their design, however, was a compromise between theatre and cinema needs as they retained stage boxes which took up space and had a poor view of the screen.

Let us begin with the Glasgow venues. The **Tivoli** in Anderston was re-built in 1904 using part of the external walls of an earlier music hall. The architect was James Thomson of Baird & Thomson, a firm best known for the remarkable cast iron Gardner's Warehouse in Jamaica Street. Three years later, it became the **Gaiety** cinema when leased to J. J. Bennell's BB Pictures Ltd.

The **Palace** in Gorbals Street was a variety palace of breathtaking flamboyance. As with the comparatively austere Wellington Palace (see above) it had been a temperance hall run by the Good Templars' Harmonic Association. In 1903, the hall was sold to Thomas Barrasford and Rich Waldon, who already ran the neighbouring Royal Princess' Theatre. Because Waldon was to run both theatres, the Palace also shared the Royal Princess' columned façade. That meant most of the budget could be spent on a fabulous interior. In the late Victorian period, people were fascinated by motifs from the far reaches of the British Empire, and so Bertie Crewe devised an astonishing Indian-inspired scheme. Yet, for all

Above: The ornate auditorium of the Palace Theatre (Bertie Crewe, 1904) in Glasgow's Gorbals. (Bruce Peter collection)

Right: A 1960s view of the façade of the Coliseum (Frank Matcham, 1905) in nearby Eglinton Street. (Tony Moss collection, CTA Archive)

Below: The auditorium of the Coliseum, viewed from the proscenium and clearly showing this large ABC-owned cinema's theatrical origins. Note that there are no seats in the upper balcony as patrons sat on the edges of the steps.

(Scottish Screen Archive)

its splendour, and an ingenious management, the course of history was to go against the continued success of theatres like the Palace. When the First World War became a national effort, the Palace, already well equipped with a projection box when it opened, was leased to Walter Thompson's Picture House Syndicate. The new policy was for cine-variety but, whenever a popular film came, the 'live' section of the show was dropped to fit in more performances of film. In 1930, the projection box was moved to behind the balcony when talkie equipment was installed and the increasingly sporadic variety element was finally abandoned. Mrs Ann McCready remembers the Palace in latter cinema days in the 1950s:

'It was advertised as 'The BEST in the DISTRICT', but the Palace still looked and smelled more like an old theatre. You went in a narrow door with a pay box, and up or down marble steps. There were fancy railings which the kids used to hide behind. I did it myself many times because you could spy through the wee holes. It was very dark inside, but quite posh still. As a wean you wouldn't get spat at in there. If you didn't have enough money for the stalls or circle, you'd walk up to the end of the block. There was another door there by a pub with its own pay box and stone steps to the top balcony. It got a noisier crowd and you sat on the floor – up there you had to tuck your dress in so that folk didn't put their cigarettes out on it.

After years as a bingo club, the Palace was demolished in November 1977 following a serious ceiling collapse.

Only a few blocks away from the Palace was the **Coliseum** in Eglinton Street, opened in December 1905 – Moss' third theatre in Glasgow (apart from the aforementioned Empire, his firm ran the **Grand** in Cowcaddens, which also showed pictures). Once again Frank Matcham designed it. A novel feature was that there were indoor waiting rooms for all customers. In variety houses, as in cinemas, the audiences could come and go as they pleased during a show, and thus there was often a queue waiting to enter. In the Coliseum, patrons could buy their tickets at the door, go upstairs and sit in comfort until others came out. The Coliseum seated no less than 2,893. There were two very deep cantilevered balconies and the ceiling was a flattened

dome with painted panels and plasterwork peacock fans in the corners. Its South Side location, remote from the city centre, and elephantine proportions hastened its demise as a theatre and so after the First World War it became a full-time cinema, retaining full orchestral accompaniments to the silent films. It was sold in March 1925 to John Maxwell's Scottish Cinema and Variety Theatres. At first, there were few structural alterations but, once talkies arrived in 1929, the proscenium was demolished and seating extended into where the stage had been, taking the Coliseum's capacity up to 3,002 seats. The new cinema proscenium was in the then-fashionable 'jazz moderne' idiom but, to anyone looking towards the balconies from the front, it was still recognisable as an Edwardian music hall even in the early 1960s. Gordon Coombes, who controlled most of the Scottish ABC cinemas in 1951-52, recalled its atmosphere:

'The vast upper circle was quite phenomenal. To take a walk up there during a housebreak with the lights on was like visiting another world. Bottles containing suspicious liquids, more likely to be 'wee heavy' than lemonade, were being quaffed. There was much vocal interchange between patrons, generally at the top of their voices, and a constant changing of seats to visit friends in different parts of the gallery. Now and again a fight (known as a 'rammy') would develop, but no-one seemed to get seriously hurt. Everyone seemed to accept such carrying-on as a normal part of a visit [there]…'

In Bridgeton in Glasgow's East End, the former **Olympia Theatre of Varieties** (1911) still dominates Bridgeton Cross with its imposing red sandstone façade. The theatre was actually the work of an Airdrie architect, George Arthur. He designed many of the burgh's fine public buildings before being elected its Provost in 1893. Producing a large modern theatre must have proved too much of a challenge though, as he wisely sought the advice of Frank Matcham's expert firm to arrange the interior – especially necessary as the theatre was fitted onto an awkward site in a Y-fork between two arterial roads. Within, there were elegant waiting areas, and the two-tiered auditorium, which was at a 45 degree angle to the foyer spaces, was decorated in the French Renaissance manner in two shades of cream with gilding, red drapes and upholstered seating for 2,000. Altogether, it was quite a contrast with the soot-stained streets of Bridgeton and the sordid cinemas which vied for its audiences. In its early days it was advertised as 'The Clean, Comfortable Family Resort… Disinfected with Jeyes Fluid in the Interest of Public Health.' It too was sold to Maxwell's Scottish Cinema and Variety Theatres. Even such an up-to-date variety house was not entirely suitable for cinema as too many of the seats had an angled view of the screen; accordingly the old interior was ripped out in 1935 and replaced with a modern cinema auditorium (designed by McNair & Elder).

In the shipbuilding burgh of Govan, the **Lyceum Theatre** opened in November 1899. David Barclay (1846-1917), a Glasgow architect better known for his grand neo-classical churches, designed it. In contrast to his other work, the Lyceum had a flamboyant red sandstone corner entrance, projecting from the surrounding tenements of Govan Road and rising to a corbelled tower, topped by an onion dome, which became a local landmark. Inside, there was seating for 2,300, and room for a further 700 standees, making the Lyceum the largest theatre in the Glasgow area at that time. In 1902, 'animated pictures' were first presented in Govan at the Lyceum. After the First World War, it became a cine-variety venue and, later, a fully-fledged cinema, and so the proscenium was removed and the seating area extended into the stage with one large balcony in 1932. This was but a brief interlude, as the old Lyceum burned down on the night of 23 October 1937

Upper right: The entrance to the Olympia at Bridgeton Cross, Glasgow (George Arthur and Frank Matcham, 1911) in 1938 following substantial re-building from a theatre configuration to a cinema by McNair & Elder. (Bruce Peter collection)
Above: A 1960s view of Bridgeton Cross with the Olympia, by now renamed the ABC, in the background. (Bruce Peter collection)

Top right: The café in the New Savoy cinema, Hope Street, Glasgow, in the 1930s. (Bruce Peter collection)

Above: Seen here in the early-1950s, the New Savoy's impressive tiled façade (James Miller, 1911) was a Hope Street landmark. (Bruce Peter collection)

Right: The auditorium of the New Savoy shortly prior to closure in 1958. (Bruce Peter collection)

and was replaced by a modern purpose-built cinema of the same name (see below).

In Central Glasgow, the **Savoy** in Hope Street, an upmarket variety theatre dating from 1911, was converted into the **New Savoy Cinema** in 1916. Originally intended as a sumptuous rival to Moss' highly popular Empire, it was advertised as 'Glasgow's Cosmopolitan House.' Designed by James Miller, its twin-towered façade was ornately tiled, while the interior was in Louis XVI style. The double-level foyer had two handsome white marble staircases which curved upwards to a café, with its own 'Roumanian' orchestra, a stall selling chocolate, cigars and newspapers and even a telephone booth. The walls were clad in dark French-polished marquetry panels, with inlaid mirrors, and the auditorium seated 1,600 in comfortable tip-up seats.

In Edinburgh, the **Palladium** in East Fountainbridge became a cinema in 1908. The building dated from 1886 when it opened as the permanent home of Cooke's Circus. By then, under the control of John Henry Cooke, the third generation of the circus family, it had become an Edinburgh institution. Cooke was born in New York in 1836 and by the age of five was an expert tight-rope walker. Brought up among horses and ponies, his circus was best known for its equestrian spectaculars. By the turn of the century, interest in circus was waning and

with his own health declining, Cooke sold the building to R.C. Buchanan, who controlled a syndicate of variety halls and cinemas throughout Central Scotland. The Palladium did not survive the transition to sound. It closed on 13 August 1932, briefly was re-used as a circus venue, then was re-built in 1935 as a variety theatre. It finally became a discotheque, then lay derelict until its demolition during the summer of 1984.

In 1906 the Poole family brought their Diorama show from their native Gloucester to Edinburgh, where they leased the Synod Hall. The **Synod Hall** had been conceived as the Edinburgh Theatre in 1875 by a syndicate of businessmen and civic dignitaries who wanted the city to have a drama and opera house to match the finest in Europe, and so they had engaged James Gowans – a wealthy and colourful Edinburgh architect and entrepreneur who was also responsible for the Castle Terrace tenements nearby. He designed an austere and monumental frontage, punctuated by five soaring arches and executed in Craigleith stone, which magnificently exploited its position in a distant view from Princes Street. Within, Frederick T. Pilkington and J. Murray Bell decorated its auditorium. It should have been a recipe for success but architectural grandeur did not come cheaply and the owners were heavily in debt when the theatre opened in 1875. Only two years later, the venture was

The Lyceum in Govan Road (David Barclay, 1899) had a distinctive tower. The theatre was re-built several times before burning down in 1937. (Bruce Peter collection)

The Palace in Aberdeen (1898) first showed films in 1911 and was re-built internally in 1931 with a new auditorium within the existing walls. Here, it is seen in the latter-1960s. (Bruce Peter collection)

Top left: The Victoria in Dundee (William Alexander, 1887) became an important member of the locally-owned J.B. Milne circuit in 1935. This photograph dates from the late-1950s and was taken by a young Milne employee, George Millar, who diligently photographed the circuit's premises out of his own interest. (George Millar)

Top right: The auditorium of the Victoria cinema shortly before closure in the mid-1980s. (Tony Moss collection, CTA Archive)

Centre: The King's in Dundee's Cowgate (1909) became a Gaumont-owned cinema in 1928 and finally an Odeon in 1973. In this 1950s view, most of the theatrical decoration remains intact and a CinemaScope screen aspect ratio has been achieved simply by lowering the top masking and covering this with layers of drapery. (Bruce Peter collection)

Below left: The Broadway in Dundee (1912) was a smaller music hall, also converted to a cinema and absorbed into the Milne circuit. (George Millar)

Below right: The Majestic in Seagate (William Alexander, 1885) became a cinema in 1919 but was destroyed by fire in 1941. (Tony Moss collection, CTA Archive)

Top right: The Palace, Methil in the 1900s; one wonders what the local mining community thought of being directed 'to the pit' also in their leisure time. (Bruce Peter collection)

Centre: The Palace, Kirkcaldy (J.D. Swanston, 1913) quickly became a full-time cinema and was absorbed into the SCVT circuit (later ABC) in 1928. The building burned down in December 1946 and was demolished. (Bruce Peter collection)

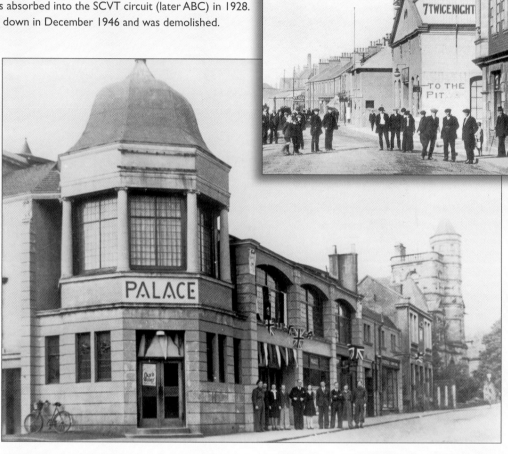

Below left: The Palace in Methil in 1950s condition, by which time the cinema was in the J.B. Milne circuit. (George Millar)

Below right: The splendidly-named Opera House in Lochgelly (1908), another J.B. Milne cinema, seen here shortly after bingo took over in the 1970s. (Bruce Peter collection)

forced to declare bankruptcy and the theatre was auctioned off to the United Presbyterian Church for a quarter of its original cost. The entire fittings and furniture were then sold to recoup the church's purchase costs before it re-opened as the Synod Hall. In 1900 it was acquired by Edinburgh Corporation and subdivided. The offices were let to small businesses and the auditorium was used for bowling, rifle ranges and by the Royal Scottish Geographical Society. Soon, Poole's Synod Hall Cinema occupied it and became one of the most popular in Edinburgh. Ironically, by the 1960s, Edinburgh's civic leaders felt that their city should have a grand opera house and so the Poole's lease was then terminated. Consequently, the Synod Hall closed in 1965 to be demolished.

The popularity of the Synod Hall made the Poole family Edinburgh cinema magnates. In 1929, Jack Poole expanded the family's business when he bought another theatre, the **Palace** in Bridge Place, Aberdeen. Its history went back to 1888 when it opened as Cooke's Circus – just a wooden amphitheatre. This later became the Palace variety theatre, run by the Livermore brothers, but it burned down in a terrible fire in September 1896. An imposing new, fireproofed and electrically lit Palace replaced it, opening two years later. The architect, John Rust, gave it a lofty if slightly crude façade – the local granite did not lend itself to ornamentation – but its commodious interior was arranged on two tiers with seating for 1,800 and colourful Venetian Gothic embellishments. Interestingly, the last bill on its opening night was 'Moving Pictures on the Electrographe' – yet another variation of the Lumière's cinematograph. When Poole purchased the theatre, it was given a radical re-build, emerging in 1931 with one large balcony and a largely-unadorned modern interior. (Jack Poole eventually had a circuit of four cinemas in Edinburgh and Aberdeen as he built the **Regent** in Aberdeen's Justice Mill Lane in 1931 and the **Roxy** in Edinburgh's Gorgie Road in 1936.)

Every single one of Dundee's theatres had gone over to cinema use by the late 1920s. The **King's Theatre** in Cowgate, dating from 1909, was perhaps the most outstanding. A local architect, James Thomson, who had previously devised the Caird Hall's imposing edifice, designed it. The King's was commissioned by a syndicate of local businessmen, styled United County Theatres Ltd. Following contemporary American practice, the balconies

faced the stage almost square-on with the single sets of boxes isolated between decorative panels on either side. This was entirely practical as from the outset it was intended that the King's should be able to present the Cinematograph and every patron would have a good view.

The **Victoria Cinema** in Victoria Road was initially the Gaiety Theatre of Varieties, dating from 1903. It was a two-tiered house with a tall, narrow sandstone frontage, designed by local architects, McCulloch & Fairley. Initially a well-found structure, over the years it was subjected to a series of destructive alterations which attempted to make the deep and narrow music hall auditorium more suitable for cinema use. In 1910, the Gaiety was enlarged with a bigger stage and improved front-of-house spaces, designed by the prolific Dundee architect William Alexander. At the same time, a projection box was added to the rear of the balcony. When it re-opened as the Victoria Theatre, run by R.C. Buchanan, twice-nightly variety bills were interspersed with film shows. Gradually, films replaced the live element and in 1935 it became known as the Victoria Cinema. The boxes were removed and the stage was incorporated into the auditorium. By the 1980s, it was so hacked about by these changes that one day its projectionist noticed alarming cracks in the auditorium. Not surprisingly, in 1989, it was condemned by the authorities and demolished.

Dundee was also well served by a series of smaller variety halls, peripheral to the city centre. The **Broadway** in Arthurstone Terrace (1912) was typical of these, it being a simple hall with a single raked floor and stadium seating to the rear. The light steel trusses, supporting its corrugated tin roof, were exposed to view. Gradually, cinema shows took over and the building was modernised to become a full-time cinema in 1938. An Art Deco pediment above the doors gave it only the slightest hint of modernity. The Broadway became a bingo hall in the 1970s and stood idle before being demolished in 1991. The **Empire** in Rosebank Street, Hilltown (1904) was of similar layout. As with the Broadway, it began with variety twice nightly at 7 and 9 o'clock, but in 1911 it became a cinema and was later sold as such to R.V. Singleton in 1927.

The **Palace** in Nethergate had begun life as an indoor circus (the obsolete circus ring was covered over by the stalls). It became a cinema in 1912, an early member of John Maxwell's Scottish Cinema and Variety Theatres

Right: The Bellshill Theatre (1904) not long after opening. (Bruce Peter collection)

Centre: The same venue as a Gaumont-British-owned cinema in the 1950s. The staff member outside is holding a measuring rod to enable Headquarters to assess what improvements might be needed following the neglect of the war years and post-war rationing. The loss of the canopy makes the design appear even more austere than previously. (Bruce Peter collection)

Bottom: A Lanarkshire tram lurches along Main Street in Mossend, passing the Pavilion (1912) on the right-hand side of this pre-First World War image. Note the complete absence of cars. (Bruce Peter collection)

circuit, but when it faced intense competition from purpose-built 'super' cinemas in the 1930s it reverted to being a variety theatre. Lastly, the 1,700 seat **Her Majesty's Theatre and Opera House** in Seagate – a splendid playhouse again designed by William Alexander – was re-styled **Her Majesty's Picture Theatre** in 1919, billed as 'Dundee's Luxury Kinema'. Renamed the **Majestic** in 1930, it was only to last until 1941 when it was destroyed by fire.

Elsewhere in Edwardian Scotland, theatres with cinema facilities were developed in the industrial and mining towns of Clydeside, Lanarkshire and Fife. Cowdenbeath was once known as the 'Chicago of Fife' when twenty pits worked within a three-mile radius of the town. Its **Empire Theatre** (1899) was a solid stone building with a single balcony and stage boxes, designed by John D. Swanston. Born in 1875, he was a Kirkcaldy architect and town councillor who produced designs for several fine Edwardian theatres, such as the King's Theatres in Edinburgh and Kirkcaldy (both with sumptuous Viennese Baroque interiors of operatic proportions), the **Gaiety** in Methil (1907), the **Palace** in Kirkcaldy (1913, later an ABC cinema), the Alexandra in Belfast and a new interior for the Dunfermline Opera House (1921). From 1914, the Empire ran cine-variety, becoming a full-time cinema in 1922. In Methil, an important Fife coal port, both the **Gaiety** and **Palace** theatres became cinemas. Of the two, the Palace in High Street was the less salubrious – a large sign painted on the side wall directed patrons 'To The Pit'; the irony cannot have been lost on its coal miner clientele. The Gaiety in Denbeath Road boasted rich Baroque-style plaster decorations in cream with gold leaf and shading, and so was considered slightly upmarket. This cinema closed finally in 1973 and the gutted building is now Rick's Nightclub, although its fly tower is still very visible. In Lochgelly, the **Opera House** (formerly Reid's Hall of 1908) had a simple interior with a barrel-vaulted ceiling and one balcony which resembled a picture-house from the outset.

In Lanarkshire, a similar pattern emerged. The **Rialto** in Airdrie's Hallcraig Street was formerly the **Hippodrome Theatre of Varieties**, but the building had actually started out in 1856 as the town's Corn Exchange, designed by James Thomson. A bingo hall since 1962, it has an attractive harled frontage on a corner with a pediment, flanked by chimneys and topped with the town's crest. The **Pavilion** in Graham Street was converted from a roller skating rink in 1911. It was a basic brick shed with one level of seating (the 'balcony' was a few steps up from the stalls) and a shallow stage (only 16 feet deep).

Larkhall, a mining town south of Motherwell, had the **Empire**, which still stands in a largely unaltered state. A pioneering venture by George Urie Scott, it was a typically sturdy brick hall with a small stage (no fly tower). Inside, there was a single raked floor with wooden forms, a barrel vaulted ceiling and pilastered side walls. There were two performances nightly with films shown on four nights from 1917. The Empire became a full-time cinema when talkie equipment was fitted in 1930. Inevitably it is now a bingo hall and is a fascinating reminder of a lost era in popular entertainment. The type was common in smaller towns across Lanarkshire: the **Pavilions** in Wishaw and Mossend (both 1912), the **Empires** in Shotts (1912) and Coatbridge (1914) and the **Olympia** in Blantyre all followed the pattern. In Bellshill, a town with several mines in its neighbourhood, the **Bellshill Theatre** in the Main Street opened in 1904 with variety shows twice nightly. It became **The Picture House** in 1911 and the structure still survives, housing shops and a snooker club. As with this venue, the majority of these structures were of perfunctory design.

The finest group of provincial theatres, however, was designed by Alexander Cullen, an architect from Hamilton, who was one of Scotland's leading exponents of Art Nouveau. Perhaps because he did not work in the city, his buildings have not attained the prominence of contemporaries like Mackintosh or Burnet. Cullen, born in 1857, was a partner in Cullen, Lochead & Brown. He was a superbly adaptable and prolific designer who could also produce houses, churches, municipal buildings and hospitals of equal quality and conviction. From 1902 to 1904, he not only designed but also invested in three important theatres for the Edinburgh city councillor and impresario, Robert C. Buchanan. With remarkable initiative and foresight, Buchanan was one of the first Scots to realise the economies of scale of having a large chain of theatres in smaller towns which alternated between offering grand opera, drama, light entertainment and variety shows presented by touring companies. In the 1890s he set up an office in London to book acts from the prestigious West End theatres to send on tour in Scotland. While in the South, he attended the

Lumière Brothers' pioneering cinema show at the Polytechnic Hall in Regent Street and quickly realised the potential of cinema as a supplement to variety bills. The **New Century Theatre** in Motherwell (1902) was the first and most interesting of the Buchanan-controlled theatres designed by Cullen. This was followed by the **Grand Theatre** in Falkirk (1903) and, finally, by the imposing **King's Theatre** in Kilmarnock (1904). Buchanan also controlled the **King's Theatre** in Kirkcaldy, designed by Swanston and completed in 1904.

Inevitably, as the new craze for picture shows became much more popular and profitable than live entertainment, one by one Buchanan's magnificent theatres all became cinemas by the 1920s, but they suffered terribly in the battle for survival. Buchanan's first love was theatre, however, and so after the First World War he sold many of his picture-houses one by one to John Maxwell's burgeoning Scottish Cinema and Variety Theatres circuit (later ABC – see below). With the advent of films with sound in the late-1920s, the inadequacies of their theatre design became apparent, and consequently each was re-built along modern cinema lines by ABC's architects, Charles J. McNair and Elder (see below). Reconstruction was radical. It took three years to demolish and re-built the New Century Theatre in Motherwell. The site was excavated to a depth of 20 feet – right down to the boulder clay. Only one wall and part

of the original façade remained when it re-opened as the **Rex** cinema in 1936 with 2,031 seats in a plain, modern auditorium; there was a drawback: the partial cladding of the original frontage in brown and cream bricks ruined the building's appearance – obviously architectural botch-ups are not a recent phenomenon.

One formerly Buchanan-controlled theatre to survive in a largely intact (but dilapidated) condition until the 1960s was the **Theatre Royal**, Coatbridge (1875), designed by a Glasgow architect, W.R. Quinton. Having passed through a succession of owners, by then it had become one of the shoddier members of the George Green circuit. John Duddy, an Airdrie cinema projectionist, recalls a visit in the late-1950s:

'The Theatre Royal was the only cinema to usher its patrons up to the 'gods', which were not only terrifyingly steep but creaky as well. It was listed as a 1,000 seater at the time, but on all occasions I visited, I never saw a seat! The audience sat on the raised steps of the floor, looking at a wee screen at their feet, through a wire mesh safety fence. To make things worse, you often had to face the side because of the shape of the balcony, or had a pillar to block the view. They crammed hundreds of kids into the dark, dirty interior. Although the paint was blackened by nicotine and the chandelier had gone,

Left: The attractive New Century Theatre in Windmillhill Street, Motherwell (Alexander Cullen, 1902).
(Bruce Peter collection)

you could just make out painted panels around the screen and ceiling dome. I recall seeing Lon Chaney Snr in a re-issue of *The Unholy Three* there, billed as the man with a thousand faces...'

In Dumfries, the Georgian **Theatre Royal** (dating from 1792) was converted first to a roller skating rink through having its pit decked over with a flat floor, then to the **Electric Theatre** in 1912. The original theatre had been designed by Thomas Boyd, but was substantially re-built by the master Victorian theatre architect, C.J. Phipps, in 1876. Messrs Peter and John Stobie, local auctioneers, then purchased the building and had its interior re-configured as a cinema. Phipps' auditorium was heavily altered: the only remnant of his design was the metal circle front, straightened and re-used in the new balcony. The Electric Theatre continued as a picture-house until 1954, known locally as 'The Scratcher'. It then lay vacant until April 1959 when the Dumfries Guild of Players purchased the historic building for further use as a repertory theatre. Today's audiences sit in its little-altered 1912 cinema auditorium, but one wishes that Phipps' delightful mid-Victorian design had been left intact instead.

In Greenock, the **Alexandra Theatre** (1905), later known as the **King's**, designed by Boston, Menzies & Morton, was taken over by E.H. Bostock in 1926 and leased to Sydney Friedman, a London-based cinema pioneer from the era of travelling shows. Friedman then spent four months converting the King's to a cinema which opened on 6 August 1928 with the silent epic *Dawn*, accompanied by a full orchestra.

In Bo'ness in West Lothian, the **Hippodrome**, designed by a forward-looking local architect, Mathew Steele, and completed in 1912, is a remarkable circular building, more closely resembling a circus amphitheatre of the era. Owned from the outset by Louis Dickson, a Bo'ness businessman, it was decorated in the then-fashionable Art Nouveau style, with harled walls, a shallow domed roof and entrance porticos at each end. Within, there was a semi-circular balcony facing a narrow proscenium. From the outset, the Hippodrome was a full-

The New Century re-built with a 'moderne' brick façade as ABC's Rex cinema (McNair & Elder, 1936); the remains of the old theatre's twin towers can still be seen protruding above – a somewhat uncomfortable stylistic clash.
(Bruce Peter collection)

The King's Theatre (Alexander Cullen, 1904) also became an SCVT and then an ABC cinema. This building's frontage remains a landmark in the town. (Bruce Peter collection)

Above: The Theatre Royal, Coatbridge approaching a seedy end in the latter-1950s. (Richard Stenlake collection)

Top right: The Georgian Theatre Royal in Dumfries (1792) became a cinema in 1912. Today, it is an amateur theatre and the auditorium has not changed significantly since that time. (Bruce Peter collection)

Centre right: The Odeon in Greenock, converted from the Alexandra Theatre, first regularly showed films in 1928. It was purchased by the Rank Organisation and fully re-built in 1956. (Bruce Peter collection)

Below: An early view of the Alexandra Theatre (Boston, Menzies & Morton, 1905) with another Greenock entertainment venue, the Hippodrome, in the background. (Bruce Peter collection)

time cinema, which it remained until the 1970s when bingo took over. Following a spell of dereliction, the Bo'ness Heritage Trust rescued this historically interesting structure. Unfortunately, it did not find further use and continued to deteriorate. With enthusiastic local support for its restoration, however, the National Lottery recently has come to its rescue and it has been restored to cinema use, hosting screenings of classic films, educational activities and community events – a very positive outcome.

After the lull in construction brought about by the First World War, a number of theatres were built which truly blurred the distinction between theatre and cinema architecture. The **Alhambra Theatre** in Kinnoull Street, Perth (1922) was developed by a local entrepreneur, James Currie, as a rival to both the Perth Theatre and the few cinemas in the town. (Currie had been an electrician who joined the BB Picture Company in the early days of the medium to help maintain its travelling cinema shows.) His architect, A.K. Beaton, designed a lavish interior with marble stairs and marquetry panels in the foyers and a spacious auditorium seating 1,010 with a single cantilevered balcony. The Alhambra later became a Gaumont cinema.

The **Alhambra** in Dunfermline was similar in conception. This theatre was developed by a syndicate of local businessmen, headed by Henry Hare of the existing Opera House, and designed by John Fraser. Construction had started in 1921, but due to materials shortages it was not ready for opening until 4 August 1924. Externally, it was entirely clad in red facing brick and had a small frontage with stone dressings facing Canmore Street. The *Dunfermline Press* emphasised 'the enormous stage…with sufficient accommodation in every way to stage grand

operas, pantomimes or spectacular plays…' Shortly before launching the Alhambra, the management had a re-think and perhaps wisely decided that Dunfermline could never support two theatres, and accordingly the new building started out as a luxury super cinema, with the screen set back in the stage and surrounded by specially-painted scenery. It opened with the D.W. Griffith film *White Rose*, followed by a documentary, *The Wembley Exhibition - The Eighth Wonder of the World*, with orchestral accompaniment. Until recently, it operated as a bingo hall with its extensive stage put to good use as the no-smoking section. Since bingo ceased, it has been re-activated by an enthusiastic volunteer group for use as a live theatre and concert venue.

Cinema architecture learned a great deal from the theatre. Firstly, upmarket cinemas began to aspire to the Edwardian requirement of respectability – demonstrated by appropriately chaste and elegant decoration, rather than crude fairground baroque. On the film exhibition side, the theatres tended to provide full orchestral accompaniment of a high quality – this was far superior to even the most talented piano accompanists found in lesser cinema venues. In future, as in the theatre, most cinemas would have balconies, not only to increase capacity but also to separate the different classes of customer, thereby attracting wider cross-sections of the communities they served. Furthermore, new cinemas in city centres and the more genteel suburbs acquired commodious and well-appointed front-of-house spaces in which to wait or to partake of 'dainty tea.' Moreover, many of Scotland's larger cinemas continued to be fitted with elaborate (though seldom-used) stage facilities well into the 1930s, perhaps just in case the supply of films was suddenly halted.

Left: The remarkable Hippodrome in Bo'ness is illustrated alongside the architect and the proprietor in this postcard published to mark the building's inauguration in 1912. Today, it is immaculately restored and an interesting survivor from the cinema's early years.
(Tony Moss collection, CTA Archive)

The auditorium of the Alhambra, Perth in the early 1950s.
(Bruce Peter collection)

Centre: The Coliseum in Glasgow after the auditorium was extended into where the stage had been in 1931.
(Tony Moss collection, CTA Archive)

A recent view of the Alhambra, Dunfermline, restored back to theatrical usage following years of bingo. (Bruce Peter)

The Olympia, Bridgeton, Glasgow re-built as a cinema in 1938 by McNair & Elder. (Bruce Peter collection)

The Regal (ex King's Theatre) in Kilmarnock after similar reconstruction in 1937. (Bruce Peter collection)

The Picture Palaces

SHORTLY after the Kinematograph Act of 1909, Provincial Cinematograph Theatres (PCT) was formed in November of that year with a capital of £100,000 to open fifteen cinemas in cities and towns throughout Britain with a population of at least one quarter of a million. It was the brainchild of Dr. Ralph Tennyson Jupp, who had studied medicine at Birmingham then practiced in South Africa until deafness forced him to give up the profession. He returned to England where he was inspired by the cinema building activities of the London-based pioneer Montagu A. Pyke to establish a circuit of his own. He gained his financial backing from his uncle, J. J. Newbould, and from Sir William Bass, Captain Aubrey Meares and Stanley Ball. He recruited a former fellow medical student, Walter Grant, who abandoned his East Coast practice to join in the new venture which started with one room, a typist and an office boy. Jupp was the managing director with Sir William Bass as chairman, while Captain Meares was the general manager, Stanley Ball ran the film department and Walter Grant was in charge of catering arrangements. It would have been easier to concentrate on dominating a particular region. Even so, for a time PCT became Britain's earliest and most upmarket cinema chain – to the cinema what Moss' Empires were to the variety business.

In part, PCT's nation-wide development was dictated by Pyke's rapid expansion which had been confined to the London area. A gentleman's agreement was reached with Pyke under which he restricted his circuit to the capital while PCT built elsewhere. The first PCT cinema opened in Dublin on 9 April 1910, seating just 220. Before the end of the year, others had followed in Manchester, Birmingham, Glasgow and Leicester, all called 'The Picture House' and seating from 350 to 850. J. R. Naylor and G. H. Sale of Derby were the company's appointed architects for its first batch of cinemas.

From the start, PCT offered continuous performances, then practically unknown, and sought expensive city centre locations, providing a standard of luxury and elegance designed to attract the 'carriage trade' – affluent middle and upper class patrons who would not have been keen to patronise the average early cinema. PCT provided seats throughout – there were no benches at the front. It was soon a cinema trade in-joke that if you wanted to reach a PCT cinema all you had to do was to ask for the centre of the town and you would find it at that very spot.

The Picture House in Glasgow was built behind the appropriately grand neo-Regency façade of what had been a furniture emporium at 140 Sauchiehall Street. It had once hosted vaudeville acts and an animated peep-show (along the lines of Walter Wilson's Colosseum – see above) as an additional lure to would-be customers. Lord Provost Sir John Ure Primrose opened the new cinema on 19 December 1910. The *Glasgow Weekly Programme* previewed the ceremony, and described the cinema's appointments:

'To enter into details of the magnificence of this new place of entertainment would be beyond the limits of our space, but we would just like to say a few words on the subject. The front entrance of the building is ornamented by Doulton ware; the seating accommodation is arranged in one central group with wide lateral aisles, the ample spacing giving exceptional comfort. There is a Balcony to which access is gained from the Lounge, accommodating

The frontage of The Picture House in Glasgow's Sauchiehall
Street (1910) not long after the Second World War.

(Bruce Peter collection)

150. There is also a promenade behind the seats luxuriously furnished with settees. The Lounge will be a special feature and is intended for use of patrons of the Balcony…

Regarding the pictures themselves, we understand that all pictures shown will be entirely new and have never been used before. The greatest care will be taken so that all elements of vulgar sensationalism will be discarded. The pictures shown will portray every kind of subject, and a special feature will be made of current and local events, episodes of interest and importance being shown within a short time of their happening. Everything that could possibly be done for the luxurious comfort and convenience of patrons is being done here, from the providing of Refreshments, Cloak Rooms, etc., to a parcel office, where visitors may send parcels free of charge to await their personal call.'

Several months after its opening, the attractions available at the Picture House continued to draw enthusiastic attention from such critics as *The Bailie* (3 May 1911) which noted that 'The Wedgwood Tea Lounge of the House is one of the pleasantest resorts to spend an idle half-hour within the boundaries of the city.'

So successful were these premises that at the first annual general meeting in February 1911 PCT declared a dividend of 10 per cent. Profits in the year ending 31 January 1911 had been £4,334. During 1911, further PCT cinemas were opened in Leeds, Belfast and Bristol, plus second halls in Dublin and Manchester. For the year ending 31 January 1912, trading profits had soared to £47,104 and more than four million people had bought tickets from PCT. Profits for the year ending 31 January 1913 leaped to £61,652. The thirteen cinemas operating by April 1913 were valued at £380,080.

For smaller privately-owned operators, emulating the grandeur of the finest picture palaces was financially straining. Architects and decorators working in the expanding cinema supply business soon realised that using standardised components could lessen these costs. Thus, the **Cinema Picture House**, which opened in Glasgow's Renfield Street in December 1911, had a grand, Regency-style façade of white faience – a shiny earthenware facing which was more resistant to urban grime than stone dressings and could be hosed down.

The auditorium of The Picture House, Glasgow in 1912. Note the charioteer above the screen opening and murals in the arches along the side walls. (Bruce Peter collection)

Moreover, it was easily moulded into ornate patterns (unlike stone which had to be skilfully carved) and an entire façade could be manufactured in a factory and sent in pieces in a railway wagon, which saved time and site costs during construction. The Cinema Picture House belonged to Glasgow Picturehouse Ltd and was designed by Neil C. Duff – a talented designer of many cinemas and churches mainly around Glasgow and the West of Scotland in the Edwardian period. Shortly thereafter, Duff completed another cinema – the **Empire** in Titchfield Street, Kilmarnock – and this had a very similar façade to the Cinema Picture House, obviously made by using the same moulds. Both cinemas had single-storey stadium-type auditoria containing just over 600 seats. Obviously, Glasgow had far greater audience potential than Kilmarnock, so in 1920 the Cinema Picture House was enlarged. Its auditorium was extended further back along Bath Lane and doubled in height to incorporate a balcony, and a second storey with a bay window was inserted into the façade, while otherwise retaining all the elements of the original design. It re-opened as the **Regent,** with the seating capacity more than doubled to 1,314.

In 1912, **La Scala** opened almost directly opposite PCT's Picture House in Sauchiehall Street. It too was a converted warehouse (which explains the excess of windows in its sandstone frontage) by Neil C. Duff and James McKissack (of John McKissack & Son). McKissack and Duff had previously specialised in churches, but went on to design cinemas almost exclusively. McKissack's cinema designing career had begun around the time of the Kinematograph Act when he converted a shop unit and back premises in Glasgow's Lauriston

Right: Union Street and the foot of Renfield Street in Glasgow in the 1920s with the white terra cotta frontage of Cranston's Cinema De Luxe in the middle distance.
(Bruce Peter collection)

Far right: The Regent cinema in Renfield Street (Neil C. Duff, 1920) following re-building from the Cinema Picture House in 1920. (Bruce Peter collection)

Above: Crowds gather in front of La Scala in Glasgow's Sauchiehall Street (Duff & McKissack, 1912) in this 1920s view. The grand department stores and trams give the city a feeling of prosperity and cosmopolitan elegance. (Bruce Peter collection)

Far left: The Cinema Picture House, later the Regent, in its original configuration.
(Bruce Peter collection)

Left: The Empire in Kilmarnock had a very similar façade – both were assembled as kits from pre-fabricated blocks of moulded terra cotta.

(Bruce Peter collection)

district into the **Eglinton Electreum**. In addition, he was a film and cinematography enthusiast himself who acted as an advisor to Miss Cranston, the famous tea-room owner, when she opened a cinema in Renfield Street in 1916. (**Cranston's Cinema De Luxe** was incorporated into a larger building by James Miller which contained tea-rooms, billiard halls and offices as well.) It appears that a third designer, John Ednie, decorated La Scala's interior with the then-fashionable mix of Arts and Crafts and Art Nouveau elements. (Ednie may have worked with Duff on other cinemas of the Edwardian era and he himself designed the rather less salubrious Hampden Picture House in Westmoreland Street, Govanhill, completed in 1920.)

Incidentally, Glasgow Photo Playhouse Ltd, which owned La Scala, was actually a sister company to Glasgow Picturehouse Ltd and shared the same directorate, a ploy to reduce tax liability.

La Scala had a large entrance hall with a carved wooden pay box, from which a warren of passages and stairways took patrons into an airy rectangular auditorium. A balcony with side slips was supported on columns which undoubtedly spoiled the sight-lines for customers in the rear stalls, but *The Glasgow Herald* of 18 October 1912, recording the opening, noted the otherwise excellent appointments:

'At the rear of the central gallery, commanding an excellent view of the screen, boxes have been fitted

… There are tea-rooms and tea lounges both in the area (stalls) and in the gallery (balcony) so situated that patrons can enjoy the entertainment while partaking of the refreshments.'

It was thought romantic to take high tea while watching a film, and the tea-rooms with their shaded lighting soon became popular with courting couples. As *Scottish Country Life* noted in 1928, this feature became the outstanding attraction of La Scala:

'When the theatre was opened, one heard the remark that its catering department would not pay. That prophecy has been entirely falsified as the café at La Scala has proved a most popular rendezvous not only with residents in the city but also for their country cousins. It is a decided advantage for busy people to have luncheon or tea and at the same time to see what is being portrayed on the screen…'

PCT felt it necessary to outdo this upstart rival, and so only two years after opening **The Picture House** was re-built along even more opulent lines. The highlight of the enlarged building was its Palm Court foyer, with a fountain, goldfish pool and cages of singing birds, so evocatively described in *Scottish Country Life* magazine:

'The Palm Court might have been taken bodily from the palace of some Roman noble of the rich Augustan

The Palm Court of The Picture House in Glasgow after re-building in 1912. This was among the most ambitious cinema interiors of the pre-First World War era. The decoration was carried out by Guthrie & Wells, a well-known Glasgow firm of interior designers.
(Bruce Peter collection)

days. With its lofty marble pillars, spacious staircases and rounded balcony, its regal carved fireplace of white marble, its mosaic floor and garlanded dome, it makes of itself a lovely picture... while the greenery of its palms, the subdued colours of its tapestry panels and the lights gleaming in its silver chandeliers afford further charming features as a setting for the warm kaleidoscope of life and movement in the place.'

The auditorium, approached up flights of marble steps, was now every bit as opulent. Seating capacity was increased from 1,140 to 1,600. Though narrow and tall by later standards, it was commodious and richly decorated in a cream, pale green, lilac and gold paint scheme, designed and executed by Guthrie & Wells, a Glasgow firm of interior decorators. Above the proscenium, there was a Roman chariot in deeply

moulded, gold-painted plaster apparently driving vigorously towards the audience. This was a cinema to compete on equal terms with the grandest theatre or music hall. (The dignity and charm of the surroundings did not impress everyone though. The marble fountain in the entrance hall proved too much of a temptation for boisterous students who enjoyed throwing one another in, and so the water displays were dispensed with when the foyer was extended in 1924.)

Edinburgh's first picture palace was developed by the pioneer cinema entrepreneur Ralph Pringle (see above). His **La Scala** in Nicholson Street (1912) ingeniously occupied the shell of a former Salvation Army hall which, in turn, had formerly been a variety theatre, The Royal Princess' Theatre. La Scala was the work of Hippolyte Blanc (1844-1917), a prolific Edinburgh-based architect of French origin best known for his Renaissance-style

Above left: The white marble-clad entrance portico of The New Picture House in Edinburgh's Princes Street (Robert Atkinson, 1913) was built into the frontage of the existing Royal Hotel. (Bruce Peter collection)
Left: The auditorium of The New Picture House, converted from the hotel's banqueting hall. (Bruce Peter collection)
Top and above right: The inner and outer foyer spaces in The New Picture House. (Bruce Peter collection)

church designs. Thus, La Scala had an opulent interior with a cantilevered balcony and slips, and a panelled ceiling, adorned with delicately modelled plasterwork in French Renaissance style. Evidently, La Scala made Blanc's reputation as a cinema architect as well for a year later he produced the **West End Cinema Theatre** in London's Coventry Street, near Leicester Square, one of the most opulent and prominent purpose-built cinemas of the period anywhere in Britain (happily, this survives in almost intact condition as a restaurant). Despite tough competition from ever newer and grander cinemas, La Scala had a remarkably long and successful career; the much-altered building continued as a cinema until the mid-1980s. Even now it still exists as the New Empire Bingo Club, but only the plaster on the balcony front remains to remind customers that it was once an early 'picture palace.'

Next, Provincial Cinematograph Theatres joined the fray. In 1913, PCT-owned Picture Houses arrived in Portsmouth and Halifax, and an Edinburgh venue was also added, the **New Picture House** in Princes Street. This was converted from the former banqueting hall of the Royal Hotel, which PCT had purchased in its entirety to enable the cinema to have a prominent city centre location. While the remainder of the hotel was leased out, PCT commissioned an up-and-coming London architect, Robert Atkinson, to build a new 850 seat luxury cinema in the hall, while the Edinburgh-based George Alexander acted as site architect to supervise its construction. Atkinson was a forward-looking and distinguished man who was well connected in the London architecture scene where he later became Director of the Architecture Association School. As befitted the 'Athens of the North', the New Picture House was an essay in neo-classical style. A striking white marble entrance portico was built into the Craigleith stonework of the hotel frontage and the foyer spaces were lined with matching marble. The ornate coffered ceiling of the banqueting hall was retained in the new cinema auditorium, which had a balcony with long slips stretching towards the proscenium arch. This was thought to be a practical arrangement as in emergencies it enabled balcony patrons to make an orderly departure through fire exits which could clearly be seen on either side of the screen. As PCT's catering operations had proven so successful in Glasgow, yet another sumptuous Wedgwood café was installed above the foyer to serve luncheons and high teas, occasionally with live musical accompaniment.

Soon the Edinburgh Picture House was also facing stiff competition as in December 1913 the **Palace** cinema opened a few blocks further along Princes Street. It was one of ten new cinemas of varying quality to open in the Scottish capital that year alone and in order to compete on equal terms, it too had a large café. It was developed by a syndicate of local businessmen, headed by Messrs Lumley and McGuire (Lumley was well-known in Edinburgh entertainment circles as the owner of the Powderhall Sprint) and reputedly cost £10,000 to build and equip – a vast sum in those days. Ironically, the Palace was designed by R.M. Cameron, the architect of the Royal Hotel into which the rival Picture House was inserted.

No doubt Provincial Cinematograph Theatres benefited over such smaller competitors from the cost savings of a large and expanding organisation. It became the first exhibition company to be quoted on the Stock Exchange and during 1913 Ralph Jupp started a production company, the London Film Company, and arranged for PCT to invest £10,000 in its initial year in exchange for first call on the output. The arrangement

The Palace in Princes Street, Edinburgh (R.M. Cameron, 1913) was The New Picture House's closest rival.
(Bruce Peter collection)

started well with the commercial success of *The House of Temperley*. PCT also began planning cinemas costing 40 per cent less for smaller towns (with a population of at least 150,000), making more of the seats available at lower prices. To build these, a new company, Associated Provincial Picture Houses (APPH), was promoted in January 1914 by PCT. It was legally distinct but had the same directorate and was even bigger in capitalisation than its parent. Initially, APPH opened Picture Houses in Aberdeen, Wednesbury and Willenhall.

True to form, **The Picture House** in Aberdeen was located near the middle of the city's Union Street and was also designed by Robert Atkinson. It was entered through a shop unit with the auditorium located in the space behind. Its construction used steel framing – a technique which was to become universally standard for cinemas as it enabled rapid construction. The main advantage was that once the frames were erected, the roofing could be fitted, thus giving some protection to allow the fitting out of the complex interior to begin at an early stage. As the lightweight steel roof trusses had curved undersides to which batons were attached to carry the ceiling plasterboard, this and almost every other cinema of its period had a shallow barrel vault overhead. As with The Picture House in Edinburgh, there was a balcony with long slips.

Both the Edinburgh and Aberdeen Picture Houses radically changed the public's perception of cinemas in these cities and each precipitated further developments, this time by local entrepreneurs or syndicates of businessmen.

George A. Boswell designed **La Scala** in Dundee, also completed in 1913. It was the town's first purpose-built cinema and was located at 30 Murraygate – a busy thoroughfare in the city centre. In such areas, street

frontage was particularly expensive to buy, so cinemas often had narrow entrances with their auditoria filling out the spaces behind shops and offices. Boswell's cinema designs in particular always seemed to make best use of such constricted sites and thus La Scala had an imposing frontage clad in white faience topped by a globe. Most unusually, to make best use of upwardly-sloping land, audiences entered the auditorium at the screen end facing the audience, rather than from the rear. Nonetheless, La Scala was a commodious and luxurious building seating 1,079 with a café and a 15-piece orchestra to accompany the films.

Initially, Picture Palaces were only developed in the main shopping streets of Scotland's largest cities where a high order of service could command the maximum admission prices, but very quickly they began to spread to upmarket suburbs and provincial towns. Thus, **La Scala** in James Street, Helensburgh (1913) – another charming cinema by Neil C. Duff – joined the expanding Glasgow Photo Playhouse circuit. Cinema chains had many cost-saving advantages over smaller operations, not least in their ability to secure the most desirable and lucrative films to show.

Perhaps that is why the **Salon,** which opened at 90

The ornate white faience frontage of La Scala in Murraygate, Dundee (George A. Boswell, 1912). (Bruce Peter collection)

A 1960s view of the auditorium of the Gaumont (formerly The Picture House) in Union Street, Aberdeen (Robert Atkinson, 1914). (Tony Moss collection, CTA Archive)

Sauchiehall Street in Glasgow in June 1913, was so short-lived when its strategic location should have made it a long-term success. Certainly, the Salon was eye-catching, it being clad entirely in brightly coloured glazed tiles in Moorish style. The auditorium had a balcony. A luxurious café and restaurant, two floors high with an elaborate glazed roof and a wealth of foliage to suggest a winter garden, occupied the considerable space above the cinema. A lift was installed to encourage patrons to make the long ascent from street level. Newspaper advertisements invited the public to:

'Come to the Picture Salon, Winter Garden and Tea Lounge. Open from 11.30am till 10pm. Specialities - Afternoon Teas and Teas à la fourchette. Orchestral Music. Comfort and Attention amid Beautiful Surroundings.'

Mrs Beveridge, manager of the rival Regent cinema, recalled that by 1920 the Salon showed second-rate films and was reputedly frequented by 'women of doubtful reputation.' It closed in May 1923.

Cinema developers found Glasgow's West End in particular a difficult area in which to get a foothold. It was thought potentially lucrative but the residents were well-enough off to travel into the city centre for their entertainment and would not tolerate having

their respectability disturbed by gaudy cinema buildings or unsightly crowds. The former burgh of Hillhead (it was absorbed into the city of Glasgow in 1891) was a little different. It began to develop into Glasgow's 'Latin Quarter' after the University moved there in 1870, and its inhabitants were some of the city's staunchest film-goers.

The **Hillhead Picture Salon**, designed by Brand & Lithgow, was opened in 1913 and proved an enduring success. The long, low building was typical of purpose-built picture-houses of the period, but the quality of the detailing and the use of structural ferro-concrete frames made it exceptional. At a time when highly flammable nitrate spools were a great fire risk – and fires often caused ceiling collapses in buckling iron and steel structures – concrete proved a safer option for cinema construction. The Salon's elegant frontage was crowned with a dome under which the entrance portico was embellished with stucco garlands and even minor fixtures such as the rone pipes were ornamented with cast iron lion's head masks.

In pre-First World War days, patrons were greeted by the commanding figure of the doorman, with a waxed moustache and wearing a military-style brown uniform with gold braid. Having bought tickets they would be ushered through mauve curtains, adding to the allure and mystery of the experience, into the Salon's auditorium. Its deeply coffered ceiling and moulded plaster garlands decorating the walls were appropriately elegant. There was a small balcony at the rear above the projection box. The music of the Salon's orchestra, led by Herr Wilhelm Iff, a portly gentleman who had previously worked in the Empire Theatre in the city centre, created a tempo to suit the show. There was then a vogue for German bands

A 1970s view of the auditorium of La Scala, Helensburgh. Note that the projection box is in the rear stalls, below a small balcony (Neil C. Duff, 1913). (Tony Moss collection, CTA Archive)

The Hillhead Picture Salon, Glasgow, photographed in the 1960s. (Tony Moss collection, CTA Archive)

Above left: The distinctive frontage of the Central Hall Picture House in Inverness (Alister Ross, 1912). (Bruce Peter collection)
Above right: A general view of Academy Street in Inverness with the Central Hall Picture House prominent on the right-hand side, behind a rather quaint bus. (Bruce Peter collection)

(many Clyde steamers also boasted these) but during the First World War they went out of favour. To keep up with fashion, the Salon instead reverberated to the sound of an American jazz band whose black singer caused a sensation with such songs as 'My Curly Headed Baby'. While the band played, tea and biscuits were served from silver trays.

Nor were such innovations confined to the Lowlands. The **Central Hall Picture House** in Academy Street, Inverness was an incongruous but imposing twin-towered edifice with steeply pitched pavilion roofs and an exotic melange of Hanseatic and Art Nouveau elements, which somehow resembled a hunting lodge in the German Alps. The building had first opened on 20 December 1912, the work of a local architect, Alister Ross. Inside, it was richly ornamented with plaster swags and medallions and the single large balcony ended with small boxes on its sides.

In Scotland, as we have seen, the distinction between 'cinemas' and 'theatres' was often blurred. Many theatres were converted to show pictures, but only the Central Hall Picture House in Inverness seems to have gone the other way. As the town's Theatre Royal had burned down in 1930, the comic, Tommy Morgan, persuaded the Central's owners, Caledonian Associated Cinemas, to use it as a theatre instead. CAC was an Inverness-based circuit which expanded between the wars to take in cinemas throughout the Highlands and beyond, eventually

becoming Scotland's largest independent cinema operator. Re-named the Empire, for the next thirty-six years it was home to opera, revue, variety, pantomime, plays, amateur productions, Highland dancing competitions and even occasional wrestling matches. It was demolished in 1971 and replaced by a nondescript speculative office block.

The Cameo at Tollcross, which opened as the **King's Cinema** on 8 January 1914, is the oldest surviving cinema still in use in Edinburgh and one of only a very few Edwardian cinemas in Scotland to remain in anything like its original form. It was constructed to the rear of a tenement, designed in 1897 by Dunn & Findlay for the upper end of the rental market. Its entrance lobby and foyer took the place of a ground-floor shop unit and the auditorium was built in the shell of a former mission hall in the back court. Unfortunately, the name of the architect responsible for the conversion has not been recorded, but the elegant interior and the pricing of its tickets at 6d and 1 shilling indicate that the King's was aimed at the wealthier end of the cinema-going public.

In 1947 the King's Cinema was purchased by Jim Poole, whose family had been involved in the entertainment industry since the early 19th century, and he re-opened it on 7 March 1949 as the Cameo. It was at this point that the cinema began to specialise in the showing of European films and of superior British and

American productions – a policy continued ever since. This move was much to the delight of many Edinburgh residents, who had been calling for the establishment of a venue to show such films since 1930 and who had set up the Edinburgh Film Guild in the same year. Jim Poole converted part of an adjacent shop into a bar, which was opened by Sean Connery in December 1963. Poole continued to run the cinema until his retirement in 1982, after which it was acquired by Recorded Cinemas of London. In 1991-93 two additional screens were added in former shops to each side of the main auditorium.

The original auditorium, now Screen One, has a gently sloping floor with arcades on each side, decorated with fluted columns and Ionic capitals featuring volutes and fleur-de-lys mouldings. From these, female figures rise to support the cross-beams of the ceiling. The walls are panelled and feature ornamental plasterwork, as does the ceiling in which ventilation grilles are embellished with classical mouldings. In recent years, the Cameo has been threatened with conversion to a bar or restaurant, but local opinion has firmly favoured its retention as a cinema. It is a rare and precious survival of a picture palace from *La Belle Époque*.

In Britain and much of Continental Europe, the outbreak of the First World War quickly halted cinema construction. It was only in the 1920s that a second generation of larger and better-appointed cinemas emerged. The first post-World War 1 cinemas showed a

The Cameo Cinema at Tollcross in Edinburgh during the Edinburgh Festival in 1951 (which was also Festival of Britain year) – hence the 'Festival Cinema' sign atop the canopy in the 'Festival of Britain' typeface. (Bruce Peter collection)

straightforward design progression from their Edwardian predecessors. Very few cinemas were built in the early-1920s as the country readjusted to peacetime conditions. The **Waverley** in Shawlands, commenced on Christmas

The Waverley at Shawlands, Glasgow (Watson, Salmond & Gray, 1922) as the ABC in the early 1970s. The modern corporate name ill becomes the rather grand sandstone frontage.

(Bruce Peter collection)

Day 1922, is a fine example from the period. Built on a corner near Shawlands Cross to a design by the Glasgow architects Watson, Salmond & Gray, its weighty, red sandstone exterior, with an imposing dome over the corner entrance, looked more like a burgh hall than a cinema. The long rectangular 1,320 seat auditorium had columns along the sides and a barrel-vaulted ceiling,

On the opening day a big crowd lined Moss Side Road to see the Lord Provost, James Paxton, arrive in his limousine to cut the tape. Paxton was impressed with the Waverley, declaring it a building 'of great dignity which will no doubt effect an outstanding improvement to the amenity of the district'. (Interestingly, its architects had recently designed the Cochrane Street extension to the City Chambers, which was then under construction.) With good programming and a popular tea-room, the Waverley was a success. In 1928 a Christie organ was fitted and ABC bought the cinema in 1929. It finally succumbed to bingo in March 1973 and later became a snooker club. The building is listed.

The **Caley** cinema, opposite the Caledonian Railway's Princes Street Station and Caledonian Hotel, at the foot of Edinburgh's Lothian Road (1923), had a Renaissance-style façade of Craigleith stone and was entered through a Venetian arch. The local architects James S. Richardson and

John R. McKay designed it for a syndicate headed by Robert McLaughlin and Captain W.M Cameron. Within, it initially seated 900 in a lofty auditorium, the style of which reflected the exterior. Such was its good reputation that after only four years it was closed for a major reconstruction supervised by a Glasgow-based architect, James McKissack (1875-1940) of John McKissack & Son. Property was acquired behind shop units to the left of the Caley, and so its direction was changed to run parallel to the rear of these. The existing auditorium was incorporated to form the back section of the new one, which could accommodate 1,800 and which was also heightened with a mansard roof. Such radical re-building works were not uncommon and time was of the essence for each day of closure lost the owners money, so specialist cinema architects, such as McKissack, building contractors and decorators became highly skilled at planning construction work to cause a minimum of disruption. Cinema owners often insisted upon penalty clauses to recoup losses suffered by delays, but contractors were usually very careful to guard their reputations in what was a lucrative and close-knit business. Evidently McLaughlin and Cameron were well pleased with McKissack's work on the Caley for he went on to design a whole series of suburban cinemas for their firm during the 1930s (see below).

The Caley cinema in Edinburgh's Lothian Road as it appeared when first completed. (Richardson & Mackay, 1923). (Bruce Peter collection)

A subsequent view of the Caley after enlargement in 1928 to a design by James McKissack. (Bruce Peter collection)

While the British had been fighting the First World War, the Americans had been perfecting the art of making movies. Hollywood now had the biggest stars, the most exciting stories and seemingly limitless finance and expertise. To show off their latest epics, the major studios built chains of luxury cinemas throughout America and beyond. Metro-Goldwyn-Mayer, then considered the most glamorous studio, was able to boast 'More Stars Than Are In The Universe' and proved its status with palatial architecture. B. Marcus Priteca, a Glaswegian who emigrated to the United States, designed some of its most innovative West Coast movie theatres – such as the San Francisco Pantages (1911) and the Seattle Coliseum (1916). Priteca went on to design a series of opulent theatres for the Pantages circuit, culminating with the stunning Hollywood Pantages (1930). Thomas Lamb, another Scots émigré from Dundee, became MGM's chief architect, producing well over a hundred movie palaces, usually in flamboyant French baroque style, all over the USA. In London, he designed MGM's showcase **Empire** in London's Leicester Square, which opened in November 1928 on the site of an old music hall. Not surprisingly, British architects who became involved in cinema design in the latter 1920s copied American precedents. Some architects even visited there to study the latest examples. In Scotland, John Fairweather was to design the largest new picture palaces – each one obviously influenced by American practice.

Fairweather was born in Glasgow in 1867. Between 1882 and 1887, he was apprenticed to James M. Morris, during which time he also studied architecture in evening classes at the Glasgow School of Art and the Glasgow and West of Scotland Technical College. At first, he designed public buildings – such as Townhead Library (1906) and a number of schools for Cambuslang School Board – but early on he found cinemas to be a rewarding new area of work. His first were **Green's Picturedrome** at Tollcross in Glasgow's East End and **Green's Pavilion** in Rutherglen (both 1914). Fairweather's cinema designs are intriguing on account of their often clever planning and robust construction, also for their grand neo-classical auditoria, but none was aesthetically distinguished externally. This was surprising given that most of his clients were former fairground showmen who had previously desired demonstrative façades, but perhaps Fairweather persuaded them that their money should be expended on cinema interiors instead where their customers might best appreciate the extra effort.

The early exploits of George Green and his sons have already been described. In 1922 they sent John Fairweather to the United States to familiarise himself with the latest cinema design trends. The trip resulted, after four years of construction work, in a 4,368-seat mammoth cinema on the corner of Renfield Street and West Nile Street in Glasgow. **Green's Playhouse** was the largest in Europe at that time and was a triumph of careful planning; in addition to a cinema it contained offices, tea-rooms, a putting range and a ballroom with a reputed maximum capacity of 6,000 dancers. Everything about Green's Playhouse was larger than life; 45 companies were involved in the project, over 16,000 tons of cement were used and special girders and trusses had to be designed to support the double-tiered cinema auditorium and the ballroom above. George Singleton fittingly observed much later that:

> 'For private individuals to invest so heavily in such a marvellous project, way before the advent of talkies, must have taken great courage indeed. I always admired the Greens for their boldness; their Glasgow Playhouse was a most remarkable theatre.'

The construction of the Playhouse was supervised by George Green's sons, Fred and Bert, and was an immense personal achievement for them. The brothers were astute businessmen. Whenever possible they used Green's own employees to do the building work. Thus, showmen, usually employed elsewhere in the company, were taught plumbing, joinery and bricklaying and set to work. The scheme was so carefully budgeted that, to save on travel costs, the workers walked every day from Green's Gallowgate showground to the Renfield Street site and the many outside contractors faced stiff penalties for delayed or unsatisfactory work. Mrs Mason, the Lady Provost, opened the cinema to great acclaim on 15 September 1927 with Monty Banks in *Play Safe* as the main attraction.

Sadly, the Greens did not invest in a new frontage to complement their epoch-making cinema; the Playhouse was squeezed in between warehouses behind a staid existing warehouse and so its façade to Renfield Street was quite undistinguished while the side and rear elevations gave the strong impression of being inspired by prison blocks, but the canopy, the big advertising signs

Above: The vast auditorium of Green's Playhouse in Renfield Street, Glasgow (John Fairweather with John Alexander and Guthrie & Wells, 1927). (Glasgow City Archives)
Left: An aerial view of Green's Playhouse in the latter-1960s; the sheer bulk of the auditorium block is notable – as is the building's inherent trashiness and disastrous intrusion into the cityscape. (Bruce Peter collection)
Below: Fred Green and Charlie Chaplin at the height of their powers in the early-1930s. (Bruce Peter collection)

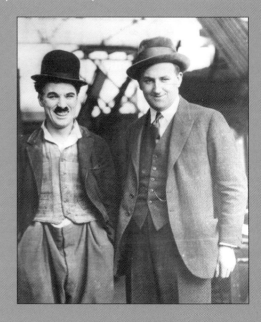

and the enormous vertical name sign, lit in American fashion by hundreds of bulbs and with the 'U' of Playhouse mounted crookedly to echo the Greens' advertising slogan 'We Want "U" In!' became a landmark at the top of Renfield Street. Massive staircases and lifts carried patrons to the auditorium, whose main decorative feature was a series of huge Corinthian columns along the side walls interspersed with boxes and supporting hefty cornices. The heavy neo-classical styling was tempered by a bright orange, primrose and gold colour scheme by Guthrie and Wells and by murals designed by John Alexander, a Newcastle-based interior decorator famous for his rich cinema projects (see below). There was a colour change lighting system and the seats were colour-coded according to their price. The projection box, crammed into the front of the lower balcony, had refreshment rooms behind it. Luxury double seats known as 'Golden Divans' in the front circle gave the best view of the screen. Watching silent films with orchestral accompaniment amid an audience of thousands, many of whom would have been smoking, must have been a remarkable experience in such a cavernous space. The films were supplemented by stage shows and the Playhouse Dancers performed new routines every week as part of these lavish programmes.

By the early 1970s, Green's Playhouse had fallen on hard times, and so it was leased to a music promoter and re-opened as the Apollo with a mixed diet of cinema and rock concerts. Having lapsed completely into disrepair, it was demolished in 1987. Incidentally, its reinforced concrete construction proved very difficult to dismantle.

The **Capitol** in Lorne Street, Ibrox might have become Glasgow's second Green's Playhouse but, as the

The former Capitol in Ibrox when briefly restored to cinema use in the late-1990s as the Bombay. (Bruce Peter)

Staff pose in front of the entrance to Green's Playhouse in Ayr in the 1930s. The manager, in full evening dress, is flanked by usherettes with the café's catering staff and projectionists to the rear. (Bruce Peter collection)

Top left: Green's Playhouse in Ayr photographed shortly after opening (John Fairweather, 1931). (Bruce Peter collection)

Greens were already overstretched to complete their Renfield Street giant, the site was sold instead to their fairground colleague and relative by marriage, Harry Kemp. Also opened in 1927, the Capitol was a massive hall on a cramped site up a side street. Externally it was unspectacular and, from some angles, ungainly. The side wall stretching along Lorne Street looked more like an engineering works than a place of entertainment. However, the Capitol's fascination lay within. Its entrance hall was small and oval-shaped and almost the entire structure was taken up by the auditorium, along whose side walls Ionic columns supported the ceiling. The colossal, 1,200 seat circle extended almost to the proscenium and the essential large crush hall occupied a space between the stalls' ceiling and the circle steppings. For some a visit to the Capitol must have been thoroughly frustrating because from seats near the side walls only the top third of the screen was visible. Amazingly, after decades as a bingo hall, it briefly became a cinema once again, named the Bombay. After only a couple of years showing Asian films, it was re-sold to property developers and demolished in favour of a block of flats.

Following on from the success of his Glasgow Playhouse, George Green next set about building a **Green's Playhouse** in Ayr to replace his existing cinema there which had burned down in September 1929. In less than two hours, the building had been entirely destroyed except for the external walls, part of the marble staircase and the front entrance, above which a notice announced forlornly 'Our Talkie Season opens on September 30th'. After clearance of the ruins, reconstruction proceeded, again to plans by John Fairweather, and on this occasion an enlarged auditorium was provided for more than 1,700 in the stalls area with a balcony accommodating about 1,300, the first six rows of which were 'Golden Divans De Luxe'. There were also four private boxes, each having settees for two, and the total seating capacity was usually quoted as 3,060. In appearance the auditorium was not unlike that of the Capitol, with ranks of Ionic columns along the side walls and with a pair of massive Corinthian columns flanking the proscenium. This Green's Playhouse re-opened to great acclaim on 8 July 1931 – the fourth largest in Scotland and equipped with a restaurant and a

The entrance foyer of the Playhouse in Edinburgh's Leith Walk as it presently appears as a theatre hosting touring productions of blockbuster musicals. (Bruce Peter)

The mighty auditorium of the Edinburgh Playhouse towards the end of its cinema days in the 1970s.
(Tony Moss collection, CTA Archive)

large stage. While the films were a big success, the stage was rarely used. Even a Frank Sinatra concert in 1953 only attracted 500 customers for two shows, out of a possible capacity of over 6,000! Green's Playhouse became a Mecca bingo hall in 1969 and as such it continues to be successful today.

The **Playhouse** in Leith Walk, Edinburgh was to be the capital's largest cinema, though it had no connection with the George Green circuit. Rather, it belonged to Playhouse (Edinburgh) Ltd – a one-cinema company set up by local businessmen. Pragmatically, they too sought the expertise of John Fairweather to draw up the plans. Behind a lumpish façade faced in Craigleith stone, this Playhouse was a truly enormous brick-clad edifice, but the planning made the best use of a steeply falling site to accommodate the auditorium and stage. The theatre was opened on 12 August 1929 with a double-feature programme: *The Doctor's Secret* with Ruth Chatterton and H. B. Warner plus *The Fleet's In*, a silent film with Clara Bow. The audience was able to admire a spacious auditorium with accommodation for 1,508 in the stalls area, 682 in the circle and an upper balcony for 863, giving a total seating capacity of 3,053. There was an exceptionally large and fully equipped stage, together with provision for an orchestra on a rising platform and a Hilsdon organ, the console of which was also on a lift.

Since closure as a cinema on 24 November 1973, the Playhouse initially had a chequered career. Those campaigning for its retention suggested that an ideal use would be as a theatre operating in conjunction with the annual Edinburgh Festival. More recently, however, it has been renovated and enjoys renewed success, mainly hosting touring productions of blockbuster musicals.

Fairweather went on to design two further giant Playhouses for the Greens at Dundee and Wishaw (see below). Moreover, his fame spread by personal recommendation throughout the fairground community and so he came to design cinemas for several other showmen who had settled down to become cinema operators – for example, the **Playhouse**, Colchester (1929) for a branch of the Bostock family, the **Picturedrome**, Burton-on-Trent for Thomas Orton (1931), the **Regal**, Saltcoats (1932) and the **Grange**, New Stevenston (1939) for Harry Kemp.

Many more picture palaces should have been built during the late-1920s and early-1930s – planning archives testify to this fact. Several proposals which did not

materialise were lodged, but cinema developers must have found it increasingly difficult to finance these ambitious schemes in uncertain times and as the adverse effects of the Great Depression began to be felt from 1929 onwards.

It has often been stated erroneously that the cinema's success and popularity was due at least in part to the effects of the Depression and that people wanted to escape from their everyday worries and dream a little. While many films of the period were undeniably escapist, transporting audiences into worlds of unbelievable luxury and ostentation as perceived by Hollywood, the Depression only had negative effects for the development of the cinema as a building type. It was very difficult to raise finance to cover the cost of developing a picture palace. Many outdated and primitive buildings from the cinema's formative years remained in business long after more comfortable and commodious premises should have replaced them. For every grand picture palace, there were several such fleapits, often with incongruously pretentious names. John Duddy, who was born in Airdrie, remembers that:

Harry Kemp's Regal in Saltcoats (John Fairweather, 1932) features large canopies – very important in the damp West of Scotland climate. (Bruce Peter collection)

'Next door to the Rialto in Hallcraig Street was **La Scala**, which occupied the old Town Hall and had ancient projection equipment. One night the picture stopped suddenly and, as usual, the audience responded with pandemonium. The chief's voice was heard through the projection porthole, shouting back "It's no a break-doon. It's <u>NO</u> a BREAK-DOON! Ma jaicket's stuck in the machine." As the projection box was built in the rear stalls, this chief had a habit of using his oil can to squirt it in the face of inquisitive heads which blocked the light path to the screen. He got his come-uppance when one evening a packet of greasy fish and chips came flying through the porthole and caught him square on his bespectacled face…

The **Garden** in Whifflet just had the screen painted on the rear wall and sound equipment made by a man called Guest. When I commented to a Western Electric sound engineer that Mr Guest never seemed to touch the inside of the amplifier, his reply was "He's frightened to – there's nae insulation on the wires in

places". Meanwhile, the entrance to the **BB Picture House** in Coatbridge was a single doorway with a narrow passage and a pay box, leading to a hall with wooden rafters and panelled walls. There were no dimmers for the house lights, so the flick of a switch put the auditorium into total darkness until the film leader began. There were no curtains either and smelly gas secondary lighting, so weak your eyes hardly noticed it…'

Primitive cinemas of this kind usually lingered on by appealing to juvenile audiences with cheaply priced children's cinema shows. Certainly, they did not offer the respectability of newer, purpose-built venues. On 31 December 1929, Scotland's worst ever cinema tragedy befell just such a venue during a matinée children's show. The **Glen** in Paisley, inexpensively converted from a Good Templars' meeting hall, had been licensed as a cinema since 1910. It had never subsequently been fitted with modern tip-up seats. Instead, it still had wooden benches without divisions which officially could seat 612 adults, or an unspecified and illegal larger number of children. Its management did not even run a proper ticketing system, and so had no way of knowing if it was exceeding its licensed capacity. Moreover, the fire exit doors were kept locked to prevent children from trying to enter without paying – a popular ruse. Soon after the first reel of a silent western, *Dude Desperado*, was finished, dense clouds of fumes began to penetrate the auditorium from the projection box. Suspecting a fire, the children panicked and rushed towards the fire exit below the screen. Unable to open it and escape, seventy children were crushed to death in the pandemonium on the stairs. The manager of the Glen was prosecuted on a charge of culpable homicide and the Glen was closed. Astonishingly, the top half of its auditorium remains eerily intact, cocooned above a shop unit.

Yet, the vast majority of cinemas were extremely well run and their managements prided themselves on the cleanliness, comfort and excellence of service they offered. The cinema's best years lay ahead and the 1930s saw an unprecedented building boom with many remarkable projects coming to fruition. For better or for worse, these new cinemas undoubtedly brought novel design concepts to the high streets and suburbs of Scotland's towns and cities.

The Glen cinema in Paisley was the scene of a terrible tragedy in which children were crushed to death. The sign is painted on in the 'jazz moderne' style (complete with sunburst), giving the thinnest veneer of fashionability to what was actually an old meeting hall. (Bruce Peter collection)

The Atmospherics

A LESS expensive alternative to the movie palace, with its marble and gilt, was the 'atmospheric' style. This involved architectural theming in any one of a number of exotic foreign manners – be they Aztec, Spanish, Moorish, Indian, Arabic, Chinese or a free mixture of any of these. John Eberson, an American interior designer, was the greatest exponent of the style. Within, an 'atmospheric' cinema would attempt to create the illusion that the audience was in a wondrous courtyard, with internally-lit three-dimensional plaster buildings and foliage adorning the walls and a smooth blue plaster sky above, complete with projected cloud effects and twinkling stars. (This had a precedent in the auditorium of the Teatro Olimpico in Vicenza in Italy, designed largely by Andrea Palladio and built between 1580 and 1585.) The films shown in atmospheric cinemas may frequently have been shot in exotic locations, or studio sets masquerading as such, but they were silent and in black and white. The 'atmospheric' cinema brought the fantasy world of the movies alive in three-dimensional colour and their exciting architecture became a part of the film-going experience.

Thus, the **Avalon** in Chicago, one of Eberson's masterpieces, was an unexpected Persian extravaganza located on a wide, arterial road, where its polychromatic tiled domes and minarets rose surreally towards the sky. It was as if part of Ishfahan had just dropped in. In its three-storey-high hallway every surface was covered in Islamic patterns of what at first appeared to be ceramic tiles but which, on close inspection, turned out to be cleverly painted plasterwork. The ceiling was encrusted with jewels of coloured glass, just like a scene from *Arabian Nights*. The auditorium was truly 'an acre of seats in a garden of dreams' – so much so that Eberson used

its design in his firm's publicity material. Beneath a glowing midnight blue sky was an elaborate Persian walled city. To one side of the proscenium, a niche contained a pilgrim's fountain. Supposedly, this had to be switched off shortly after the theatre opened as the sound of running water made customers seated in the vicinity need to visit the toilets! However, a visit to the ladies' would have been another unusual experience, for it was modelled on a harem, replete with fountains and a cool ceramic floor.

In Britain, 'atmospheric' design was briefly fashionable in the late-1920s and early-1930s, the most famous examples being the **Astorias** at Brixton (1929), Streatham (1930) and Finsbury Park (1931), designed by Edward Stone and Tommy Summerford.

In explaining the seemingly sudden vogue for 'atmospheric' cinemas, however, it must be remembered that vigorous architectural theming had remained a current in cinemas ever since their early fairground incarnations. The quasi-Egyptian frontage of the **Govanhill Picture House** in Bankhall Street, Glasgow (1926) was one of the most eye-catching in the city. Designed by Eric Sutherland, whose cinema schemes were few and idiosyncratic, the entrance was decorated with Egyptianesque columns and stripes of blue and white tiles. A scarab in moulded tiles adorned the pediment and the façade was flanked by gold-domed towers. Also on Glasgow's South Side, the **Kingsway** cinema on Cathcart Road (1929) by James McKissack had a long, gently curving façade in Spanish-American style. Both had very plain interiors, however, which did not reflect their exotic façades.

Scotland's first truly atmospheric cinema was located far out of central Glasgow – on its urban fringe, in fact –

in Knightswood, a new scheme of Glasgow Corporation-owned housing built from the mid-1920s onwards to help relieve inner city congestion. At that time, the Labour Councillor George Smith was the Corporation's housing convenor and he believed that cinemas were important social amenities which greatly enhanced such new housing developments. Smith was also an entrepreneurial businessman and a cinema pioneer. He was a friend of the Singleton family and, like R.V. Singleton, he had first organised cinema shows in 1910 in Corporation-owned halls around the city. With his business partner and fellow Labour councillor, James Welsh, he went on to develop a number of cinemas in Glasgow's peripheral suburbs during the 1930s. Both Smith and Welsh were prominent and distinguished public servants; Welsh served as Member of Parliament for Paisley in the 1929-31 period and subsequently became Glasgow's Lord Provost between 1943 and 1945.

Although Smith earmarked the site for a cinema in the Knightswood housing development, it was, however, another entrepreneur, William Beresford Inglis, an architect and property developer, who designed and operated the **Boulevard** which opened in 1928. Sited among expanses of grey-harled terraces and semi-detached villas, it was a remarkable and intricate essay in the Spanish-American style. As with many suburban cinemas developed in the following decade, the Boulevard occupied a spacious site, its entrance facing onto Knightscliffe Avenue with a long side elevation flanking Great Western Road. In city centre locations,

The former Govanhill Picture House in Bankhall Street, Glasgow (Eric Sutherland, 1926) in use as a clothing warehouse in the early 1990s. (Bruce Peter)

while forming part of a continuous high street frontage, the necessarily functional auditorium block could be screened from view. As more cinemas were developed in the suburbs, what seemed like acres of unadorned brick auditorium wall and asbestos roofing often made them potential eyesores. In contrast, the Boulevard was carefully designed to look well from all angles. For a start, it was entirely clad in white stucco which lent it a semblance of unity. There were stubby, pantile-roofed towers at each of the four corners and a mixture of tiling, stuccowork and hacienda windows adorned the frontage.

The Kingsway, Cathcart as the Singleton-owned Vogue in the 1960s. The Spanish-styled exterior design was not followed through indoors.

(Glasgow City Archives)

The exotic decoration of one of the auditorium side walls in the ABC-owned Ritz in Cambuslang (Wm Beresford Inglis, 1930). (Bruce Peter collection)

The Boulevard at Knightswood on Glasgow's Western Fringe. (CTA Archive)

Centre: The Toledo at Muirend on Glasgow's South Side, Beresford Inglis' most ambitious and convincing cinema design in the Spanish style, photographed when new in 1933. (Glasgow City Archives)

Right: The auditorium of the Toledo in the early 1980s. (Allen Eyles)

Bottom left: A 1960s view of the Toledo's entrance foyer with Spanish-styled tilework and a modern refrigerated snack and ice cream counter. (Bruce Peter collection)

Bottom right: The original proscenium with curtains featuring butterflies, flamenco dancers and matadors. (Bruce Peter collection)

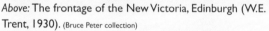

Above: The frontage of the New Victoria, Edinburgh (W.E. Trent, 1930). (Bruce Peter collection)

Top right: The New Victoria's spacious outer foyer.

(Bruce Peter collection)

Right: The stalls foyer rather resembles an ocean liner interior of the same period. (Bruce Peter collection)

Below: The rather swish café of the New Victoria – an important adjunct to any upmarket city centre cinema.

(Bruce Peter collection)

Two views of the New Victoria's rather restrained atmospheric auditorium, showing the view across the front stalls with the safety curtain in place (this is painted to depict a Roman scene) and the view from the stage with the orchestra pit in the foreground. (Bruce Peter collection)

Although its style may have been dubious, the building had sufficient visual integrity to establish Inglis as an important, if only occasional, cinema architect.

The interior was a great piece of escapism. It was an imaginative Hollywood-inspired 'take' on an Andalusian courtyard in a Glasgow housing estate. Either side of the proscenium, exotic buildings with stained glass windows, ornamental balconies, fancy wall lanterns and pantiled roofs were massed high to the blue sky of the ceiling, lit by random patterns of lights resembling stars. For sure, it was an appropriate setting for Westerns! It also reflected a new and distinct attitude to cinema design. Especially in the suburbs, such buildings – one might refer to them as 'going out' architecture – were a counterpoint to everyday existence. They offered vivid colour, romance and escapism combined with comfort. Unfortunately, 'serious' architectural commentators failed to appreciate this fact. *The Architectural Review*'s correspondent P. Morton Shand caustically dismissed one atmospheric cinema as mere 'architecturalised acoustics' and accused its designer of 'going over to the enemy' (the cinema in question was **The Richmond** in Surrey by Julian Leathart).

In 1938, the Boulevard was sold to the Singleton circuit. According to George Singleton 'Inglis said he found running cinemas too stressful and wanted to concentrate on hotels. He complained about film renters,

booking agents and problems with staff. Poor man! He seemed unaware that if anything hotels were even worse. Think of the laundry for a start!' Before that, however, he went on to design further 'atmospheric' cinemas around Glasgow. His **Ritz** in Cambuslang was the only true 'atmospheric' in Lanarkshire. The façade was dull – an arch set between shop units – but the interior again was remarkable, with three-dimensional Spanish buildings and plaster foliage around its walls. The 1,595 seater was built in 1930 for ABC and was demolished by them in 1960 to make way for shops and offices.

At Muirend, on Glasgow's southern extremity, William Beresford Inglis built his masterpiece, the superb **Toledo** (1933). A comprehensive essay in his favourite Spanish-American style, it was much more confident and cohesive than any of his previous designs. Externally, the Toledo was a glorious confection of hacienda windows, ornamental balconies and friezes. Inside, the proscenium was framed by columns and topped with pantiles. Matadors and butterflies adorned the predominantly red and purple screen curtains. Around the side walls, above dado panels bordered with Spanish ceramic tiles, whitewashed buildings with red pantiled roofs and balconies mingled with palm trees and amphoras. Viewed through arches, painted panels gave the illusion of sun-kissed landscapes with walled settlements on escarpments, disappearing to the horizon. The ceiling was

Another later and lesser Scottish project by Trent was the Gaumont in Alloa (1939), seen here after the Second World War with a measuring rod leaning on the canopy to provide a sense of scale.
(Bruce Peter collection)

a dark blue night sky. It cast an enduring spell over its patrons and continued in business, albeit in mutilated form, until October 2001.

The **New Victoria** in Edinburgh (1930), in contrast, was a severe, almost Germanic variation on the 'atmospheric' genre and was in fact similar to the Mercedes Palast in Berlin by Fritz Wilms (1926). It had a blue 'sky' ceiling and rusticated side walls with slender Ionic columns and statues of the muses in top-lit niches. The painted safety curtain depicted a Roman forum. Its designer, William E. Trent (1874-1948), was a highly respected London-based cinema architect who had previously designed many fine cinemas in England for Provincial Cinematograph Theatres, for whom the New Victoria was commissioned.

As a young man Trent was articled to Henry Poston of Lombard Street, London, with whom he remained as an assistant until 1905. While in this office, he studied at the Architectural Association evening school. In 1922, he designed the large **Super** at Ilford, which later became an important PCT cinema and may have impressed its managing director, William Evans, for he appointed Trent to be PCT's chief architect in 1925. He was then responsible for a batch of PCT Regents – Sheffield (1927), Stamford Hill in London (1929), Bournemouth (1929), Ipswich (1929) and the 1929 reconstruction and enlargement of the fire-damaged **Regent** in Brighton, originally designed by Robert Atkinson in 1921. Next, Trent designed a number of New Victoria cinemas for PCT. These were at Preston (1928), Bradford (1930) and, finally, Edinburgh. The latter was Trent's only attempt at an atmospheric design as it was built during a phase of stylistic transition between his earlier neo-classical vocabulary and his later modernistic designs. PCT was

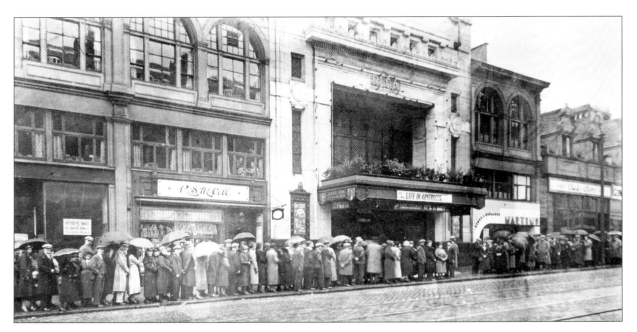

Queuing in the rain for admission to the Regal in Sauchiehall Street, Glasgow in the mid-1930s. Note the shop to the right of the cinema's entrance with a remarkable streamlined Vitrolite frontage. (Tony Moss collection, CTA Archive)

The auditorium of the Regal when first opened in 1929.

(Bruce Peter collection)

A smaller version of essentially the same design in the Regal, Hamilton (1931). (Bruce Peter collection)

taken over by Gaumont-British in 1929, but although Trent remained this firm's regular architect, he only designed one other cinema in Scotland – the **Gaumont** in Alloa (1939), which was a utilitarian effort in comparison with much of his other work. All other Scottish Gaumonts were second-hand acquisitions.

Not all atmospheric cinemas had plaster skies and fake buildings around the perimeter of their auditoria, however. The London-based interior designer Charles Muggeridge produced an alternative version of the genre, since termed 'semi-atmospheric.' Instead, his interiors were back-lit through pergolas, hung with delicate plaster foliage. Picturesque wall murals in bas relief were made three-dimensional through the liberal application of further simulated vegetation, so that the overall effect was of being seated at dusk in a lush, romantic, landscaped garden. His first and most elaborate exemplar of this approach was the mighty **Regal** at Marble Arch in London (1928). John Maxwell's ABC circuit leased the Regal shortly after it opened as a London showcase for his Associated British Picture Corporation's film releases. He must have been enamoured by its design for he commissioned Muggeridge to design the interiors of his new Glasgow flagship cinema – the **Regal** in Sauchiehall Street.

Fittingly, Maxwell purchased the former Ice Skating Palace and Hengler's Circus building at 326 Sauchiehall Street in which Glasgow's first public cinema show had occurred. After Hengler's closed in 1924, the building had become an unsuccessful ballroom called the Waldorf Palais. John Maxwell commissioned Charles McNair to convert the structure into a sumptuous cinema with the latest facilities. The building contractor was George Urie Scott's Cinema Construction Company; in partnership with McNair, it designed and built, or converted, nearly all subsequent ABC cinemas in Scotland. The Regal opened on 13 November 1929 with a 'talkie.' Invited guests saw, and heard, Al Jolson in *The Singing Fool*, which had already caused a sensation at ABC's Coliseum south of the Clyde, where it had enjoyed a record-breaking run.

The Regal was a long, five-storey building, running parallel to the street. As the site sloped steeply up from Sauchiehall Street, the auditorium had to be at first floor level with shop units and a car park below. Muggeridge decorated the interior in autumnal tones and a specially-woven carpet with a pattern of interlocking leaves was used throughout. Twin staircases ascended to the stalls

foyer from which two-storey-high windows gave wide views over the street and whose long curtains, potted palms, rattan couches and gilded plaster ceiling with ornate cornices and chandeliers created a luxurious atmosphere. There was a café and smoking lounge either side of the foyer and more flights of stairs led to the upper levels of the auditorium. The proscenium arch was tapered and perforated with organ and ventilation grilles, ornamented with plaster foliage which complemented the illuminated gold screen curtains. On each side wall a *trompe-l'oeil* autumnal landscape was viewed between high, pilastered arches. The army of usherettes, page-boys and ticket checkers were all dressed in the Regal's smart, brown uniform with gold braid and buttons; the usherettes, for example, wore a brown tunic and skirt, a black Spanish hat, silk stockings and high-heeled shoes. Every customer was personally shown to his or her seat. With the pick of ABC's releases, the Regal was an instant and enduring success with long queues most days.

Next, Muggeridge was retained to design interiors for the **Rex** cinema in Riddrie (1931), again with a shell by McNair. Riddrie was another sprawling municipal housing scheme on Glasgow's urban fringe developed under the direction of Councillor George Smith. As John Maxwell told the audience at the opening, it also 'effected a much needed improvement to the sparse amenities' of the area, and it was a great success. According to Alex Cameron, who was a customer in the early-1930s, but later emigrated to Australia:

> 'The Rex was a revelation when it opened. It had upholstered seats ... thick carpets ... and hidden lighting, luxuries we had never experienced before. It was in the Rex in 1939 that I saw the Pathé News about the impending world war. Even at the age of twelve I think I realised the anxiety caused by a possible conflict. Two weeks later I became an evacuee, never to return to Glasgow.'

The **Regal** in Hamilton, opened in August 1931, was similar to the Rex. It initially seated 1,800 and such was its success that in 1937 the balcony was enlarged to give a total of 2,023 seats. Each cinema closely resembled the Glasgow Regal with Romanesque overtones and murals of naïve landscapes flanking the screen.

The **Kelvin** cinema, located on Argyle Street in Glasgow's Finnieston district, was the result of

The auditorium of the Kelvin, Finnieston, Glasgow (Gardner & Glen, 1930). (Bruce Peter collection)

The Orient, Gallowgate, Glasgow (1932). (Bruce Peter collection)

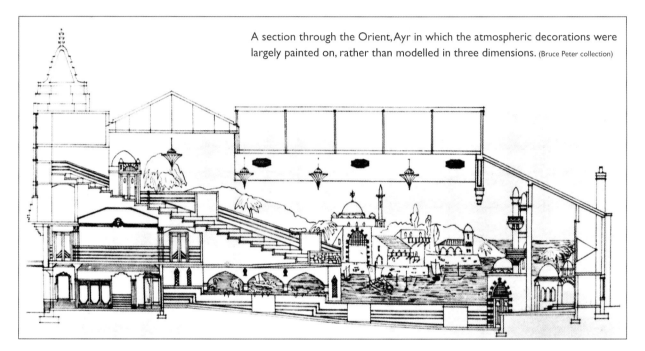

A section through the Orient, Ayr in which the atmospheric decorations were largely painted on, rather than modelled in three dimensions. (Bruce Peter collection)

Right: The Orient, Ayr in the 1990s following conversion for bingo. (Bruce Peter)

Below: The Orient, Glasgow as a bingo hall in the 1970s. (Bruce Peter collection)

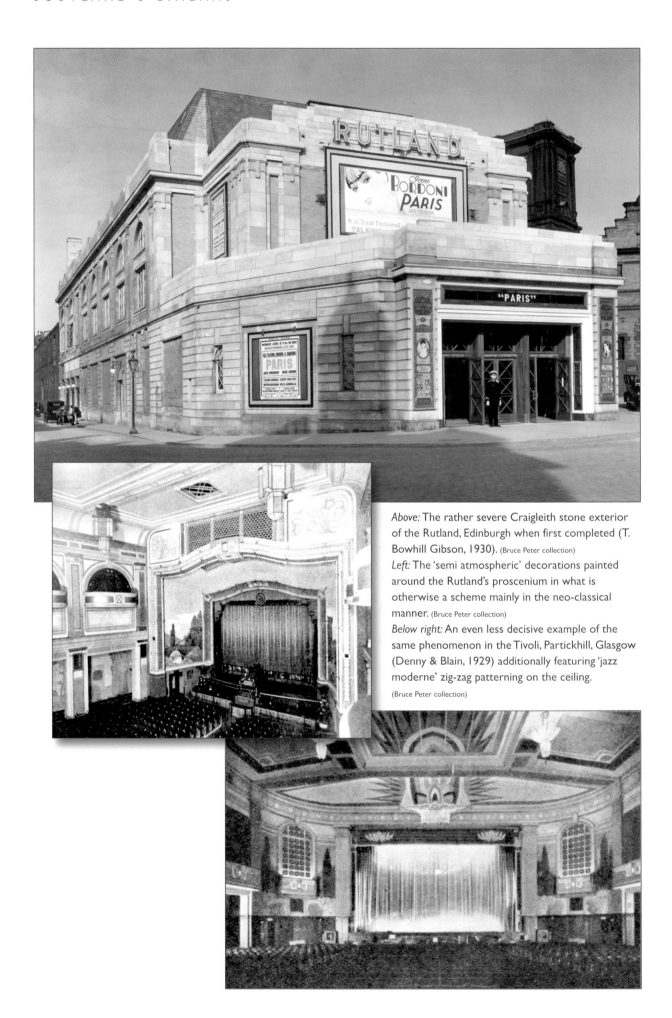

Above: The rather severe Craigleith stone exterior of the Rutland, Edinburgh when first completed (T. Bowhill Gibson, 1930). (Bruce Peter collection)

Left: The 'semi atmospheric' decorations painted around the Rutland's proscenium in what is otherwise a scheme mainly in the neo-classical manner. (Bruce Peter collection)

Below right: An even less decisive example of the same phenomenon in the Tivoli, Partickhill, Glasgow (Denny & Blain, 1929) additionally featuring 'jazz moderne' zig-zag patterning on the ceiling.

(Bruce Peter collection)

collaboration between the architects Albert V. Gardner and William R. Glen. Gardner, the older of the two, was an eccentric designer who had designed a number of early Glasgow cinemas such as the Partick Picture House (1912). His partner, Glen, was a graduate of the Glasgow School of Art who had commenced in private practice in 1904, joining up with J.A. Campbell and A.D. Hislop. Glen was involved in the building of the Queen Victoria Memorial School at Dunblane, presenting the special trowel to King Edward VII for laying the foundation stone. He then served in the First World War in the Glasgow Highlanders, reaching the rank of major and winning the Military Cross. His partnership with Gardner followed.

Completed in 1930, the Kelvin was a bizarre mixture of geometric forms and multiple roof levels with an octagonal stair tower at one corner. The auditorium in this extraordinary edifice was clad, roof and walls, in asbestos panels. *Bioscope* magazine's description of its 'admirable – and thoroughly Scottish – combination of the practical and the artistic' was incredible considering that the Kelvin's interior was devised in a semi-atmospheric manner with a Turkish mosque on one side of the screen and a Spanish scene on the other. The Kelvin initially belonged to Kelvin Cinema Ltd of which John Maxwell was a director, and Maxwell's ABC booked its films for the first two years. After failing to acquire outright control of the Kelvin, Maxwell withdrew from its board. The Kelvin closed in 1959 and has changed hands several times since. After a spell of dereliction it became the Crème de la Crème, which claimed to be the world's largest Indian restaurant though, unfortunately, none of the atmospheric interior decoration remained. That venture closed in 2005 and the former Kelvin was demolished.

Gardner and Glen split up shortly afterwards as Glen was invited by Maxwell to come to London to set up an architect's office in his Golden Square headquarters and take charge of ABC's new building programme. Gardner remained in Glasgow, where he designed further 'atmospheric' cinemas.

In Glasgow's East End, the **Orient** (1932) was a spectacular confection; a weird and wonderful ziggurat tower, adorned with geometric Art Deco motifs, capped its entrance on the corner of Gallowgate and Sword Street. The foyer and vestibule were capacious and dominated by a sculpture of an amazon on a plinth set into the circle staircase. Elaborately decorated, brightly painted cornices and pilasters gave a foretaste of the spectacular 'atmospheric' treatment within. A warren of dark passages, waiting areas, ante-rooms and stairwells had to be negotiated before emerging into the ponderous 2,500 seat auditorium with its large, horseshoe-shaped balcony. In the distance across a sea of seats, the proscenium was formed by an arched bridge in plaster resembling rough-hewn stonework and painted overall in gold, beneath which the screen curtain depicted a landscape with a castle on a hill. On either side Gardner had produced cute Spanish and Norman fantasylands with gates and turrets all made of plaster and lit from within. In the 1960s it became a bingo hall, which continued until 1995. An elderly bingo customer there recalled that:

'During the thirties the Orient offered excellent value for money; the doors opened at 6.30 pm every night and audiences could see a double feature, recent newsreels, cartoons and a documentary before it closed at 11 pm – all for 5d (2p)! It was very busy, though it rarely got films on their first release. Months after they had toured the suburbs, big epics like *The Prisoner of Zenda* would be shown. Sometimes the prints were a bit worn and flickery but the place would be filled to the last seat. These were hard, cramped and squeaky. The Orient was never in the luxury class but, by Jove, it had tremendous atmosphere.'

No doubt the Orient's highly embellished interior design also contributed to this feeling of well-being and the perception among patrons of being generously rewarded for their custom.

Also in 1932, Gardner designed a smaller sister **Orient** cinema in Ayr. It too was an outlandish design in which the décor was given a Moorish theme. On a narrow site, the possibility for three-dimensional treatments in the auditorium was restricted and so originally there were miniature buildings in three dimensions only around the proscenium, while those on the side walls were painted using false perspective on the flat plasterwork. These atmospheric effects were swept away in the 1950s when the interior was re-built to accommodate wide-screen CinemaScope. After passing through a string of owners, the Orient became a bingo hall in 1983. It is now a night club.

In pre-war years, visiting Campbeltown, near the foot of the Kintyre Peninsula, made a pleasant day's sail by steamer from Glasgow. There, the **Picture House**, located on the waterfront, was re-built by Gardner in 1934 and became a miniature version of his other exotic cinema schemes. It had originally been opened in 1913, but is still in business today and claims to be Scotland's oldest continually working cinema. Inside its tiny auditorium, there are fake plaster castles on either side of the screen with a multitude of lights in the ceiling, but only slightly reminiscent of a starry night sky. It remains a quaint and charming building with almost a Shangri-La quality.

Very quickly, the 'atmospheric' cinemas became very dated – not least because, following the arrival of 'talkies' in 1929, the unpredictable acoustics caused by their three-dimensional auditorium walls with their miniature buildings and plaster foliage made them highly unsuitable. Moreover, the advent of spoken dialogue in films greatly increased the possibilities of the cinema as an entertainment medium. Previously, in the silent era, the picture palace had been an entertainment complex in which the films themselves were only one component, it presumably being thought that silent films were not enough of an attraction in their own right. While comfort was an important factor in their success, the total experience of escapism – the fantasy of the films shown, the glamour of the grandly costumed performers on stage, the equally impressively costumed cinema staffs and the exoticism of the cinema building itself – all contributed to a feeling of well-being in their audiences and, no doubt, left them feeling that they were receiving good value for money.

While 'atmospheric' cinemas at least displayed some totality of vision, the vast majority of cinemas from the late-1920s and early-1930s more often than not displayed a hotch-potch of vague ideas. Sometimes apparently random mixes of differing styles were thrown together. The **Tivoli** in Partickhill, Glasgow (1929) was typical. Designed by William J. Blain of Denny & Blain, a Dumbarton-based firm, its façade treatment and interior plasterwork were in chunky Roman classical style, but this was overlaid with 'atmospheric' touches – such as unsophisticated landscapes painted between the pilasters on the auditorium walls. The ceiling, in contrast, was adorned with vibrant 'jazz moderne' zig-zag sunbursts in primary colours. The **Rutland** in Canning Street, near Rutland Place in Edinburgh (1930), by T. Bowhill Gibson, was a similarly heavyweight neo-classical design, but once again this was tempered with painted scenery in the auditorium. There was desperation to find a new and appropriate look to distinguish cinemas properly from theatres and to signal their growing importance as venues of the fastest-growing and most progressive entertainment of the period.

The Super Cinemas

IN 1928, the 'talkies' arrived in Britain, a new word for a new experience. Technically, films with added sound were not a new idea as in 1907 a film of the variety star Harry Lauder with a synchronised sound-track on a record had been shown at the Hippodrome theatre in London's Charing Cross Road. Warner Bros used their Vitaphone system to add sound to *The Jazz Singer* with Al Jolson (1927), which was released in Britain the following year, and *The Singing Fool* (1929). 'Talkies' gave the cinema new potential and audiences grew bigger than ever.

The first Scottish cinema to be purpose-built for 'talkies' was the **Ritz** in Rodney Street, Edinburgh, opened in September 1929 and designed by Albert V. Gardner and William R. Glen. Moreover, it was one of the first entirely new Associated British Cinemas properties. Hitherto, John Maxwell's cinema circuit had expanded through the purchase of existing cinemas and entire circuits. It was only with the advent of talking pictures that he turned his attention to developing new purpose-built premises, although second-hand acquisitions continued. In these circumstances, one might have expected the Ritz to be a memorable building, but actually it was an edifice only notable for its dullness. Gardner and Glen split up shortly afterwards (as has been described above). Glen was invited by Maxwell to come to London to set up an architect's office in his Golden Square headquarters and take charge of ABC's new building programme.

ABC went on to open over a hundred new cinemas during the 1930s. The firm and its sister companies in film production and distribution were one of the unqualified success stories of British business in general during a difficult decade. The Associated British group

Above: ABC's Ritz in Edinburgh's Rodney Street is advertised as 'The Sound Cinema' in this image taken shortly after it opened in 1929. (Bruce Peter collection)
Right: The Ritz's auditorium was typical of cinemas of the period.
(Tony Moss collection, CTA Archive)

grew larger and larger, making profits and paying good dividends every year. At that time, making money from cinemas was not difficult but the firm also indulged in film production successfully (i.e. without losing money) – a skill which eluded Gaumont-British and was not even attempted by another later competitor, Odeon. By 1937, Associated British Cinemas could claim to be the second largest cinema circuit in the world (the American MGM subsidiary Loew's was the biggest) and it was certainly far ahead of the Gaumont and Odeon chains (which were then under separate ownership). At its peak, ABC sold nearly six million tickets a week. With an excellent spread of well-located cinemas, it was screening a generous proportion of the best Hollywood pictures as well as its own products. With its blue and red triangle trademark, ABC became a household name for almost every film-goer in Britain.

The advent of talking films in 1929 led to a great expansion of interest in cinema and new buildings proliferated throughout the country. The 3,002-seater **Astoria** in Glasgow's Possil Road was enthusiastically promoted in the cinema trade press as 'the largest working class sound kinema in the world' when it opened in 1931. Yet, it was more of an engineering marvel than

a visual feast. Architect Albert V. Gardner's biggest-ever project, the fan-shaped building was erected on the site of a filled-in quarry. Excavation to a depth of thirty feet was necessary to allow the foundations to stand on solid rock, and the sheer size of this 6,000 square foot mammoth meant that it took sixteen months to build – a long time in cinema construction terms. Externally, the Astoria was an ugly brute and a disastrous intrusion into the cityscape. It presented vast monotonous flanks of grey roughcast walls, perforated with prison-like windows and capped with an industrial-style asbestos roof, dwarfing a dull two-storey entrance portico. Only its name sign, held in mid-air by a metal framework, gave any impression of its purpose as a place of entertainment.

The interior, in the 'jazz moderne' idiom, was recorded by *Building Industries* magazine:

'The vestibule is octagonal in shape, as is the box office, which stands in the middle of the space. The colour scheme… is very brightly carried out. From the entrance hall one sees on the first landing a very effective rising sun motif in gold, green and red…The auditorium decoration is carried out in modified futuristic fashion with a shade of marigold

The Astoria in Possil Road, Glasgow in the late-1950s shows the rather industrial appearance of this very large inner city cinema. Note that there are special shows for teenagers being advertised with banners around the cupola. (*Bruce Peter collection*)

predominating... the design of the ceiling is emphasised by four large cubist lights, suspended to form a square and with a huge, brightly coloured inverted cone slung in the centre. The sun decoration is enhanced by grotesque figures on the side walls...'

What the Astoria lacked was any sense of visual cohesion or co-ordination. This highlighted a gulf in cinema design between the modernity of the latest technical equipment and servicing – heating, ventilation, sound systems and projection – and new aesthetic developments in other areas of architectural practice – such as factory and exhibition design. Cinema designers badly required a new language to achieve better visual integration, while communicating to cinema-goers the desirable qualities of modernity, luxury and escapism.

The prominence and decorative eclecticism of cinemas certainly made them vulnerable to criticism and they incurred the wrath of pro-modernist architecture critics and practitioners, such as Philip Morton Shand and Maxwell Fry who were already looking to the recent German developments of the *Bauhausler* and the expressionists, such as Eric Mendelsohn, and demanding a purer architecture which would amply reflect and emphasise the modernity of the cinema medium. Shand, in particular, was so incensed by what he considered the inability of British architects to follow the trends set by Continental modernists that in 1930 he published a book, *The Architecture of Pleasure: Modern Theatres and Cinemas* to show how much better he felt contemporary German cinema design in particular was than its British counterpart:

'The newer ad hoc buildings often vie with one another in that *nouveau riche* ostentation which their patrons are invited to envisage as 'the last word in luxury'... The design of our cinemas is part of the heavy price we pay for our public neglect of architecture... The desire of the film exhibitor being usually to disguise his picture theatre as a showman's booth, it is not surprising that British architects have so far had no adequate chance of trying to discover the cinema's most logical and satisfactory structural form...'

While his chosen illustrations with hindsight show that he was a man of advanced taste, at the time it was perhaps too advanced for the majority of the British audience. A glance through Shand's book reveals how influential German cinemas of the 1920s were to become on British cinema designs of the following decade. The book was part of the process of raising aspirations, as were articles and illustrations in the various architectural journals.

A seminal building in this debate was the **Titania Palast** in Berlin opened in 1928. Designed by Ernst Schöffler, Carlo Schloenbach and Carl Jacobi, this important landmark cinema design on a prominent corner site was split into different volumes building up in mass towards the entrance, which was surmounted by an elegant, fin-shaped tower. It was at night that the Titania Palast made its most important visual statement, as its different volumes were boldly outlined in coloured neon strips, while its tower glowed with bands of light. The graphics of the cinema name were carefully chosen to enhance the design. The new possibilities offered by the sudden and widespread commercial availability of neon effects lighting were exploited first by the Germans (hence Lichtspielarchitektur). For cinemas, which uniquely housed a light-based entertainment medium, this provided an appropriate new visual language. Besides, most customers would be visiting them at night, when neon embellishments and floodlighting suffused them in warm glow and made them welcoming beacons on the high street. These innovations made a virtue of the self-advertising nature of cinema; the German architects recognised that lettering and display should form an integral part of the design and not just appear as an afterthought.

Perhaps the greatest of the German cinemas of the 1920s was the **Universum** on Kufurstendam, also in Berlin, by Eric Mendelsohn (1928). As the most prominent component in a larger development of shops, offices, a hotel and flats around a new shopping plaza, the Universum had a horseshoe-shaped auditorium with a continuous circulation space around its perimeter (necessary in the cold North German winter climate). This was boldly expressed in the sweeping lines of the exterior form, one element being piled on top of another in receding layers. The prow-like fin was emphasised by parallel lines to carry advertising and dramatically pin-pointed the entrance. In the auditorium, no ornamentation was allowed to distract the audience and lighting troughs in the side walls and ceiling focused the eye towards the screen – it was perhaps the first 'machine for viewing movies.'

In addition to this cinema, Mendelsohn won large commissions for offices and department stores in the bustling hearts of Berlin and other large German cities where his bold expressionist designs addressed contemporary life and the consumer society. While some modern architects focused on industrial imagery and standardised construction, Mendelsohn excelled at making industry's effect upon urban life thrilling rather than threatening. He was an artist and an intellectual who made several trips to America, first travelling there in 1924 with the film director Fritz Lang. Both became fascinated by the massive scale and dynamism of the American metropolis. Subsequently Mendelsohn sought to bring these qualities of light and movement to his architecture. By substituting lettering and lighting for allusions to the past, he invented a more democratic and alluring commercial architecture, animated by sleek curves and elegant details which celebrated, rather than attempted to disguise, the new consumerism of the 1920s. Mendelsohn's staccato description of his Universum cinema expresses the qualities of his architecture:

'Thus no rococo palace for Buster Keaton,
No stucco pastries for Potemkin....
But, also no fear!
No sober reality, no claustrophobia of life-weary brain

acrobatics,
Fantasy!
Fantasy ...dominated by space, colour and light.'

In May 1930, Mendelsohn lectured at the Architectural Association and at the Architectural Club in London. With the growth of anti-Semitism in Germany, he moved to London in 1933. His arrival in Britain was a pivotal moment for the development of the Modern Movement; his leaving Germany signalled the end of expressionism in German architecture and his arrival in Britain and subsequent designing of the De La Warr Pavilion at Bexhill-on-Sea began the vogue for the approach here. The product of a widely publicised competition, the Pavilion offered dramatic evidence of the lightness and openness possible with the new style.

In England, the **New Victoria**, adjacent to Victoria Station in London, was the one of the first and certainly the most prominent British cinema to be influenced by Continental modernism when it opened in 1930. Its architect, Ernest Wamsley Lewis, had studied at the Architectural Association School from 1920 to 1925 under Robert Atkinson. In 1927, he won a travelling scholarship to study theatre design in America and Germany. On his return, he set up practice and was engaged by William Evans, the managing director of Provincial Cinematograph Theatres, to design this trend-

Left: The New Victoria in London (E. Wamsley Lewis, 1930) drew on German practice and influenced the design of subsequent British cinemas. (Bruce Peter collection)

Right: The extraordinary auditorium of the New Victoria when first completed. This has survived well and still delights audiences today who visit to enjoy musicals. (Bruce Peter collection)

The lighting sconces on the side walls of the Playhouse in Elgin (Alister G. MacDonald, 1932) demonstrate the influence of the New Victoria – albeit in an otherwise more conventionally rectilinear space. (Bruce Peter collection)

setting cinema. When William Evans asked Wamsley Lewis what the decorative theme for the interior would be, he replied 'a mermaid's palace'. The main inspiration was Hans Poelzig's Grösses Schauspielhaus in Berlin. Illuminated columns burst into great stacks of plaster shells with glowing internal lighting – 3,000 concealed bulbs lit the interior; notwithstanding such careful attention to detail, its final cost worked out at £189,000 and not the £250,000 budgeted. It became clear that a progressively styled cinema was not only quicker to build but also much cheaper than a traditional 'picture palace' with its expensively treated materials and time-consuming craftsmanship. The New Victoria was widely publicised in the architectural press and even *The Times* used it to illustrate an article about modernism entitled 'Revolt in Architecture.'

Shortly afterwards, the **Playhouse**, Elgin (1932) appeared. It was one of the first cinemas inspired by the Modern Movement to be completed in Scotland. Its interior design certainly owed a great deal to the New Victoria, with which its architect, Alister G. MacDonald, was personally familiar as he had attended its opening

night. MacDonald (1898-1993) was the son of the Labour Prime Minister, Ramsay MacDonald. He was well-connected, widely travelled and cosmopolitan. Having studied at Slade School of Art and Bartlett School of Architecture, both parts of the University of London, he joined the office of the cinema and theatre architect Frank Verity as Clerk of Works in 1926. This introduced him to cinema design and it may have engendered an interest in film, for at the end of the decade he left for New York to study skyscrapers, then continued to Hollywood to examine lighting and acoustics on film sets. This indicates his growing interest in building science, which was to prove useful in the 1930s when he designed a number of innovative cinemas on awkward sites. Apart from his architectural pursuits, MacDonald, the son of a famous father, was evidently a success on the Hollywood social scene. He made friends with Charlie Chaplin, whom he invited to Chequers to meet his father when he next came to Britain. Later, MacDonald travelled to Italy to study a marsh drainage scheme near Rome. There, he met Mussolini and was invited to collaborate in designing a skyscraper in Milan – an offer which was tactfully declined.

Back in Britain, in 1932 MacDonald was commissioned by Caledonian Associated Cinemas to design a number of new cinemas, of which the Playhouse in Elgin was the first. CAC, as it was known, had its head office in Inverness and its properties were concentrated in the Highlands, along the North-East coast between Inverness and Aberdeen, with subsidiaries in Fife, East Lothian and the Borders.

The **Angus Playhouse** in Montrose followed in 1933. Whereas the Elgin cinema was entered through an existing shop unit and therefore had no façade of its own, the Angus Playhouse had a long frontage with the auditorium running parallel to the street. MacDonald's treatment of this exterior also showed the New Victoria's influence. His elegant and inexpensive volumetric design seamlessly tied the tapering auditorium into the foyer block with smooth coloured render and bold horizontal lines. The staircase was emphasised by a tall window, while the interior made use of layered plasterboard, the shadows of the edges picked up by concealed lighting. The Playhouse had 1,059 seats, including a fully cantilevered balcony and tea-room, all for only £15,000. It closed in 1977 and was subsequently demolished. MacDonald went on to design the **Playhouse**, Peebles (1933) for CAC, followed by the **Broadway** in Prestwick (1935) and the **Lyceum**, Dumfries (1936). The latter's interior was also very similar to that of the New Victoria, albeit on a smaller scale. (Back in London, MacDonald produced a series of ingenious newsreel theatres, the finest of which were located on the concourses of the Victoria and Waterloo railway stations.)

At the same time, CAC appointed a Kingussie-based architect, Colonel Alexander Cattanach (with advice from T. Bowhill Gibson), to design a further batch of new cinemas which included its flagship property, the **Playhouse** in Perth (1933). Astonishingly, this 1,700 seater was completed in only nine weeks from laying the first brick – a feat which *The Ideal Kinema* magazine considered a record. Five years later, Cattanach more or less repeated this design for the **Regal** cinema in Rothesay, which eventually joined the CAC circuit too.

The **Capitol** in Aberdeen became a progressive design almost by accident. Aberdeen Picture Palaces, the local circuit controlling most of the cinemas there, had learned that a rival firm, Poole's from Edinburgh, was planning to build a large cinema in the city centre (the Regent). As this would cream off the best of the new releases by offering film distributors more seats to fill, and hence potentially more profits (films were hired on a percentage basis), Aberdeen Picture Palaces felt obliged to trump Poole's project. Opened on 4 February 1933, the Capitol was described in *The Aberdeen Press and Journal* as 'the Cinema in Excelsis'.

The Playhouse in Perth (Alexander Cattanach, 1933), seen here in the 1970s, set a record for fast construction and the building still remains in cinema use today. (Bruce Peter collection)

The similar Regal in Rothesay, completed in 1938, was a prominent building on the popular Clyde resort's promenade. (Bruce Peter collection)

The neatly detailed exterior of the Angus Playhouse, Montrose (Alister G. MacDonald, 1933). (Bruce Peter collection)

The Angus Playhouse's auditorium; the walls are finished in layers of plasterboard with lapped joints to cast shadows in a regular pattern. (Bruce Peter collection)

The Broadway, Prestwick (1935) has a symmetrical frontage with streamlined wings. A large café was located above the entrance foyer. (Bruce Peter collection)

The spacious auditorium of the Broadway, making use of concealed lighting around the ceiling perimeter and the proscenium. (Bruce Peter collection)

The Playhouse in Peebles had a similar auditorium to MacDonald's Montrose cinema, completed the same year and for the same owner, CAC. (Bruce Peter collection)

A rendering of the interior of the Lyceum in Dumfries (1936). As with the Elgin Playhouse, this shows the influence of the New Victoria. (Bruce Peter collection)

The frontage of the Capitol in Union Street, Aberdeen, clearly showing the very elegant entrance doors with their half-circular glazing and chrome work and also the neat graphics above. (Bruce Peter collection)

The Capitol, outlined with neon and floodlit from the canopy, attracts a large crowd on its wet and cold opening night in February 1933. (Bruce Peter collection)

Centre right: The Capitol's balcony ladies' powder room was pure Hollywood with Art Deco make-up tables, bevelled mirrors and a jazzy carpet. (Bruce Peter collection)

Below left: The rather hotel-like balcony foyer, adorned with potted palms and poster boards showing the screen idols of the period. (Bruce Peter collection)

Below right: The Capitol's simple but stylish auditorium, which remained intact until the late-1990s before being trashed to form two night clubs. (Bruce Peter collection)

A local architect, Clement George, had already produced plans for a cinema on Union Street in 1927 and, as this was almost directly in front of Poole's site on Justice Mill Lane, it seemed ideal. George was asked to revise his design to make it as large as possible and he took the project with him when he went into partnership with one of Aberdeen's most distinguished architects, A. Marshall MacKenzie, in 1931. Shortly, Clement George's health began to fail and he died in February 1932, leaving MacKenzie's firm to complete the Capitol. The job architect was a recent graduate from the Architectural Association in London, David Stokes. For new graduates, the early-1930s was a difficult time to find jobs in the architectural profession, and so Stokes was fortunate to be employed, even if that meant travelling nearly from one end of Britain to the other. By chance, therefore, this most prominent city centre cinema project fell into the hands of Stokes, a young man who was heavily influenced by the Modern Movement (he had attended lectures by Eric Mendelsohn and other forward-looking Continental architects while at the Architectural Association). Throughout Britain, the cinema building boom was to employ many such graduates who were interested in modernist principles. (Interestingly, Marshall MacKenzie's son, Alexander G.R. MacKenzie, was the partner in charge of the firm's London office, which had opened in 1902. There, he undertook a number of large commissions – such as the Waldorf Hotel on Kingsway – and was a respected figure on the London architectural scene. It may be that Stokes initially sought work there, but was re-directed to Aberdeen instead).

Clement George's fairly conventional and undistinguished plans were subjected to a bold reworking from which the Capitol emerged as an entirely new design that was strongly influenced by German practice. The existing Union Street frontages (which George had intended to keep) were swept away and replaced with an elegant new flat granite façade, the centrepiece of which was three tall windows, rising to a pediment and outlined at night with blue neon and floodlighting. Blue and silver tones were used throughout because Aberdeen was, after all, 'the silver city by the sea', and the style was set by four sets of entrance doors, with modish stainless steel semi-circular windows and hand plates. These formed fully circular 'targets' when the doors were closed.

The foyers and auditorium were symmetrical and in line. The outer foyer was panelled in polished teak, while the inner vestibule was at mezzanine height and was dominated by the balcony staircase, with its tubular steel railings and flanking stairs down to the crush hall for the stalls. The walls curved into the ceilings and there was little superficial decoration. The auditorium, in pale blue, made use of Holophane – a patented type of coloured effects lighting – which was concealed behind coves to suffuse the space in ever-changing colours. As a city centre cinema on an important thoroughfare, the Capitol had a restaurant, full stage facilities and a cinema organ. Such adjuncts were generally dispensed with as the 1930s progressed and more cinemas were developed in the suburbs, but in town and city centre sites a restaurant or café was still a sign of refinement. These facilities offered elegant surroundings in which to enjoy luncheons and 'dainty teas' and were noted for courteous service and reasonable prices. Thus, they became respectable havens for ladies meeting for a lengthy chat, and for children accompanied by mother meeting elderly aunts over a pot of tea. One of the Capitol's most intriguing features, however, was its ladies' powder room, accessed off the balcony foyer, replete with bevelled mirrors, fluted make-up tables in modish black, cream and mint green and a stylish Art Deco carpet.

The Capitol was much admired in the architectural press and it was included in the Royal Institute of British Architects' centenary exhibition, International Architecture 1924-1934, in London as an example of best practice. As a cinema and, later, a theatre it was an enduring success and, apart from repainting in warmer pink and gold hues, was little altered since that time. Most unfortunately, notwithstanding being a listed building, it has recently been cruelly subdivided to form a series of night clubs. This reconstruction has destroyed

The Astoria, Kittybrewster, Aberdeen shortly after opening in 1935. (Bruce Peter collection)

Above: The design of the auditorium may have been inspired by the success of the nearby Capitol. This image shows how it looked when first opened. (Bruce Peter collection)

Left: The Majestic in Aberdeen's Union Street (Thomas Scott Sutherland, 1937) had rather a lumpish façade in granite, as shown in this 1970s view. (Tony Moss)

its spatial integrity and much of its architectural interest.

Elsewhere in Aberdeen, the architect and business entrepreneur Thomas Scott Sutherland (born 1899) later designed the **Astoria**, Kittybrewster (1935) and the **Majestic**, Union Street (1937), but these ponderous granite edifices lacked the sophistication of the earlier Capitol and neither survives today. Despite having only one leg, Sutherland was a hard-working and prolific man who was also a director of thirty-nine companies, including the Inverness-based Caledonian Associated Cinemas circuit.

By the early-1930s *The Glasgow Herald* was speculating that Glasgow had reached saturation point with cinemas, but the fact that existing ones were consistently well attended stimulated ever grander schemes. A British subsidiary of the American Paramount Corporation commissioned its favourite British architects, Frank T. Verity and Samuel Beverley, to design central Glasgow's first entirely new, free-standing cinema, the **Paramount,** which was to be the city's most lavish super cinema. Verity and Beverley were highly regarded for their magnificent Italian Renaissance style theatres and cinemas, such as the Paramount in Paris and the Plaza in London. Later, in collaboration with an American interior decorator, Charles Fox, they designed spectacular Art Deco Paramounts in Newcastle, Leeds and Manchester but the new Glasgow theatre was to be modern. A complete block between Renfield Street and

West Nile Street was cleared in just seven weeks and a towering façade of cream-coloured reconstructed granite (specially treated to resist urban grime) was built along Renfield Street and curving round the corner into West Regent Street. Above its entrance, there was a canopy surmounted by five tall windows, separated by fin-shaped mullions. The most extensive display of neon lighting on any building in Scotland was carried round the façade and along both main street fronts and a six-foot-high neon name sign in elegant cursive script dominated the skyline. Glasgow had never seen a piece of architecture quite like it.

Inside, the Paramount was even more extraordinary, but before being allowed to discover its splendours customers had to buy their ticket from an external pay box, an American peculiarity. Passing through the vestibule, they entered a two-storey-high entrance hall, with a grand staircase leading to balcony level, whose walls were covered in panels sculpted with a bewildering array of Art Deco motifs lit from above and below. Throughout the theatre, ceiling coves concealed around 40,000 light bulbs which illuminated the spaces in slowly changing colours. A staff of almost 200 was employed not only to see to customers' needs but also to maintain the place.

Upstairs were the Balcony Café and Paramount Restaurant. The latter was two floors high and positioned over the main entrance to use the light from the five tall

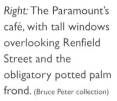

Left: The balcony foyer of the Glasgow Paramount. (CTA Archive)

Right: The Paramount's café, with tall windows overlooking Renfield Street and the obligatory potted palm frond. (Bruce Peter collection)

The Paramount in all of its neon-lit glory and ready for the opening night in December 1934. (CTA Archive)

Left: The Paramount's ornate Art Deco auditorium – note the organ console on display to the left of the orchestra pit. (CTA Archive)

Below: Another view of the Paramount's auditorium, looking towards the screen tabs from the balcony's rear section. (Bruce Peter collection)

windows in the façade. Rattan chairs, white linen table-cloths and swathes of curtaining combined with specially-designed carpets and subdued lighting. The auditorium seated 2,784 and was decorated in copper, green and silver. An automatic vacuuming system was connected to a central cleaning plant to 'scientifically clean the entire theatre several times a day'. There was a large stage and several dressing rooms for variety programmes. Audiences thrilled to the music of a full orchestra, the strains of a Compton organ with a silver console and the dancing of a troupe of Tiller Girls.

Opened by the Lady Provost, Mrs A.B. Swan, on 31 December 1934, the Paramount immediately became one of the busiest cinemas in Scotland and the most frequented Paramount outside the United States.

Perhaps fearing that Britain would be overrun by German forces, Paramount sold its UK circuit in batches to Oscar Deutsch's Odeon chain between 1939 and 1941. The acquisition was a major coup, giving Deutsch luxury cinemas in city centre locations, the very thing he had postponed building himself on account of cost. The Glasgow Paramount was shortly renamed **Odeon**, which it remained for nearly seventy years thereafter.

Green's Playhouse in Dundee (1936) was easily Scotland's most spectacular cinema of the 1930s, yet it also presented one of the most schizophrenic stylistic contrasts. As the cinema was built on a site sloping down towards the River Tay with its street frontage restricted to a space no wider than a shop unit at its top end on Nethergate, a spectacularly-designed façade was required to gain maximum publicity from such a narrow opening. According to Tommy Green, there was an obvious choice as architect:

> 'When Joseph Emberton began designing pavilions for Blackpool Pleasure Beach, in which the Green family had shares, they also sought Emberton's services as he realised that a cinema with a modern exterior would be an immediate attraction and would give his patrons a glimpse of the future.'

Moreover, one of Emberton's assistants at that time was George Fairweather, John Fairweather's nephew.

Born in Audley in Staffordshire in 1889 and the son of a draper, Emberton joined the local Potteries-based architects Chapman & Snape at the age of seventeen. In the evenings, he studied at Burslem Art School, from

which, aged 22, he won a scholarship to study at the Kensington College of Art in London. Upon graduation, Emberton joined the firm of Trehearne & Norman, engaged in designing several of the large neo-classical-style office buildings along Kingsway – Central House, Imperial House and Regent House. At the same time, he made the acquaintance of Thomas Tait, a partner in Burnet, Tait & Lorne, which had recently completed the Egyptian-style Kodak House (1911), also in Kingsway.

During the First World War, Emberton served with the Honourable Artillery Company in Egypt, where the vernacular plastered mud buildings fascinated him. After the War, he joined Tait's office, before going into partnership with the shop and exhibition designer Percy Westwood. In 1925, Emberton visited the *Exposition des Arts Décoratifs* in Paris, which caused the style of his work to change once again. Decorative ironwork and Lalique glass details soon began to adorn shop facias he designed for Austin Reed and others. Later, by the mid-1930s, the most obvious influence on Emberton's work was that of Eric Mendelsohn, whose De La Warr Pavilion at Bexhill-on-Sea was the perfect model for the pavilions he subsequently designed at Blackpool Pleasure Beach.

For Dundee, Emberton created the tallest tower on any British cinema, rising 85 feet in sheer white render and glass. At night, it was outlined in red neon with a blue 'waterfall effect' of timed neon flashers behind the name sign. The foyer was a great expanse of cream terrazzo with sycamore floor-to-ceiling panelling and troughs of light in the ceiling to emphasise its scale. On Sundays, when cinemas were not allowed to open for film performances, the tables and chairs from the adjacent cinema café were moved into foyer and the carpet in the café itself was then rolled up to reveal a maple dance floor so that the Playhouse could still make money as a venue for tea dances. Its *café-dansant* was reputedly then the most fashionable and elegant resort in Dundee.

In complete contrast to its Emberton exterior, it had a palatial 4,114 seat auditorium designed by John Fairweather and decorated by John Alexander. As in Fairweather's previous Playhouses, this was lined with ranks of soaring Corinthian columns which stood clear of the walls with the side aisles behind. Alexander's contribution appears to have consisted of Art Deco grills with fountain motifs on either side of the proscenium and a colour scheme in shades of gold. Two levels of private boxes filled the spaces between the two bays closest to

Left: Green's Playhouse in Dundee (1936) had a vast tower facing Nethergate, designed by Joseph Emberton. In this 1960s scene, Elvis Presley is the big attraction. (Bruce Peter collection)

Top right: The spacious foyer of Green's Playhouse with a generous expanse of terrazzo flooring leading to a grand staircase. (Bruce Peter collection)

Centre right: The 'Café-Dansant' at Green's Playhouse, also the work of Emberton. (Bruce Peter collection)

Below right: The auditorium, by John Fairweather with decorations by John Alexander, in a mixture of neo-classical and Art Deco styles. (Bruce Peter collection)

Above: Staff flank the Dominion's pay box which is decorated with chrome trim and acid-etched glass.

(Bruce Peter collection)

Left: The Dominion, Morningside, Edinburgh (T. Bowhill Gibson, 1938) – a luxury cinema in an upmarket suburb.

(Bruce Peter collection)

Right: The auditorium of the Dominion, Morningside, shortly after being completed – the epitome of an upmarket 1930s suburban cinema.

(Bruce Peter collection)

Bottom left: The County cinema in Portobello (T. Bowhill Gibson, 1939).

(Bruce Peter collection)

Bottom right: The auditorium of the County, Portobello, when first completed.

(Bruce Peter collection)

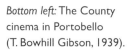

the stage and the ceiling had a vast saucer-dome. A sound structural logic informed this design solution. Beneath their ornate moulded plaster coverings, the columns contained robust framing which helped to brace the side walls, enabling them to support the vast and weighty balcony and ceiling girders. The junction between Emberton's streamlined foyer and Fairweather's mainly neo-classical auditorium was handled with a broad white marble balcony staircase featuring illuminated balustrades to make a 'fountain of light' effect, rather like the more famous example in the foyer of the Strand Palace Hotel in London, designed by Oliver Bernard and now preserved in the Victoria & Albert Museum.

The Playhouse's eclectic design shows how the diverse decorative impulses of cinema architects, decorators and proprietors continued in the 1930s. Writing about recent cinema architecture in *Architectural Design and Construction* in March 1938, A. Calveley Cotton observed:

'Clients and architects are fluttering indecisively between old 'styles' and 'adapted modernism' in an attempt to discover what the general public like... Every component used in the building of a cinema, the choice of architect, site, picture renting, sound installation and decoration, is employed to one end only and that is to draw the general public past the pay box, and the enticement of the public must be done as a paying proposition...

After this somewhat depressing primary consideration there is another aspect which has to be considered which divides the cinema interior decoration world into two schools of thought: (a) one which holds that decoration is more effective when it is executed purely as a theatrical set or romantic scenery, and (b) the other more modern school which relies on the simple shock tactics of big lighting troughs, streamlined plenum grilles and smooth lines. Most architecturally-minded people who have not a great deal of knowledge of the cinema world would undoubtedly agree with the second school of thought. But the public are not fooled into thinking that they are entering a portion of old Egypt, nor do they worry why such colourful Gothic architecture should suddenly appear inside a modern building. The public doesn't come out to be educated but the public does appreciate that someone has taken pains to provide a very sumptuous, pleasant and cheerful

harbour from the cold and wet of the sometimes dismal surroundings...'

By the mid-1930s, Scotland's city centres were well served by several generations of cinemas, and so, from then on, the majority were developed in suburban locations and in larger provincial towns. For reasons of cost and speed, in such places only modernistic designs were considered. Moreover, many Scots felt a positive affinity with modernity as it was regarded as being synonymous with the aspirations of a progressive, industrial nation. Scottish cinemas of the latter 1930s, however, exhibited a more pronounced 'chunkiness' than their English counterparts. Typically, they had pitched roofs concealed by deep parapets, harled or brick exteriors (in Scotland Vitrolite glass was never used as a facing for cinemas, but was popular in England for this purpose), fewer windows (none had the expanses of Crittall glazing found in the frontages of many English cinemas) and thicker mullions. This was certainly not due to ineptitude on the part of their designers in coming to terms with the latest construction techniques; rather, it was a pragmatic response to a harsher climate. (After all, modern buildings by respected 'mainstream' Scottish architects were similarly robust-looking – for example Gribloch, near Kippen, by Basil Spence and Thomas Tait's housing at Silver End in Essex, a factory village developed by Crittall.) By then, a Scottish cinema architecture 'establishment' was in place – a number of specialist practitioners who knew exactly what their clients expected.

In Edinburgh T. Bowhill Gibson (1895-1949) designed a small number of important cinemas around the city and beyond. The **Dominion** (1938), located on a side street in Morningside, a well-heeled and genteel district on Edinburgh's South Side, was handsomely appointed and enduringly successful. It was faced with panels of Craigleith stone and had a commodious interior which made good use of Holophane lighting. The **County** in Portobello (1939) had a tall façade with flanking drum towers in artificial stone, between which there soared a tall advertising fin which was glazed with glass blocks and illuminated from within by colour-change effects lighting, while the rest of the façade was lit by neon and flood-lighting. The County was promoted by Henry Paulo and Robert Scott – the former was of fairground origin and the latter was a local businessman.

Above: The Raith in Kirkcaldy (James McKissack, 1938) after conversion from a cinema to a ballroom in the 1960s. (Tony Moss collection, CTA Archive)
Right: The Embassy in Troon (James McKissack, 1937) also had a distinctive cloud-shaped façade. (Bruce Peter collection)

Edinburgh was not an easy place for would-be cinema developers. Its city centre was already densely developed. The Old Town had few large enough sites to be worthwhile and the Georgian New Town was a *fait accompli*, and so most projects in the 1930s served newly-built suburbs, be they municipal or private developments. James McKissack designed a couple of medium-sized super cinemas for various subsidiaries of Robert McLaughlin's circuit to serve Edinburgh's new peripheral housing estates – such as the **Carlton**, Piershill and the **Embassy**, Pilton. He also designed the **Raith** in Kirkcaldy, Fife for the same owner. While the former two were conventional to the point of dreariness, an idiosyncratic cloud-shaped entrance portico distinguished the entrance to the Raith. McKissack gave a similar treatment to the **Embassy** in Troon, designed for another of his important clients, the Ayrshire-based K.R. Blair circuit (which also ran cinemas in Irvine, Beith and Girvan). Altogether, McKissack worked mainly for four cinema proprietors, located right across Central Scotland. His most important designs were for Glasgow-based circuits.

That city had been in perpetual expansion since the Industrial Revolution and in the 1930s it increased further with new garden suburbs of bungalows for the middle classes and further municipal housing schemes to relieve inner city congestion. Glasgow was regarded by the film industry as 'Cinema City' and the Cinema Exhibitors Association established that the average

Glaswegian must have gone to the cinema a staggering fifty-one times a year to achieve the attendance figures recorded in the late 1930s. This is remarkable as some people, particularly in prosperous areas, rarely if ever went to see a film, preferring the city's many live theatres; the others simply went several times a week. With 139 cinemas in business at the outbreak of the Second World War (Edinburgh had only 65), Glasgow could boast more cinema seats per head of population than any other city in the country and these were evidently occupied more often than those in Manchester, the city with the next highest ratio.

In Glasgow, McKissack designed exclusively for the Smith & Welsh and Singleton circuits. Smith & Welsh, it will be remembered, were Labour Councillors and Smith was the city's Housing Convenor. Whenever a new municipal housing development was built in the 1930s, a cinema for Smith & Welsh to a McKissack design was subsequently erected on a prominent adjacent site; this was entirely legitimate, enabling residents to enjoy their leisure time in environments of reasonably good quality. (Alas, features such as cinemas were lacking in Glasgow's less successful post-war council housing schemes.)

McKissack's other main client, George Singleton, was a man of advanced ideas. Describing his first purpose-built cinema, the **Broadway** in Shettleston, Singleton explained his own philosophy about cinema design:

'We found a site just off Shettleston Road. It was cramped and on an awkward corner and James McKissack was asked to make a very conspicuous entranceway that could be seen from Shettleston Road. It didn't matter what it looked like as long as it was eye-catching and everyone could see that it was there. He did us proud. James Welsh chose the name to match up with his other halls and it had the right Hollywood feel. I was very proud of the Broadway. It was my first big achievement when I went into the cinema trade and it cost £30,000; not much in today's terms may be, but a great deal then.'

The Broadway was indeed dominated by the prominent corner portico ordered by its owner; almost three storeys high, it was clad in stripes of blue and cream tiling. As to the interiors, which were largely unornamented:

'We never felt that ornate decoration would be needed because we always showed films in continuous performances and usually started them before the audience was allowed in, so they rarely saw the auditorium with the lights on. This trick also spared electricity and in that respect our cinemas were ahead of their time as simple interiors became standard practice for everyone later in the thirties…'

The Commodore at Scotstoun in Glasgow (James McKissack, 1933) began as a Singleton-owned cinema, but was quickly sold to Odeon. This had a twin-towered frontage in green, cream and orange faience. (Bruce Peter collection)

McKissack went on to design further Singleton cinemas – the **Commodore**, Scotstoun (1933) and the **Vogue** cinemas in Rutherglen and Strathmartine Road, Dundee (both 1936). That September, Singleton sold his entire

The Broadway in Shettleston, Glasgow (1930) was somewhat less well resolved but, as it was located up a side street, the majority of customers would hardly have seen the bulk of the auditorium. Here, it is seen in post-war guise as the Odeon.
(Allen Eyles collection)

Top left: The Odeon (ex Vogue) in Dundee's Strathmartine Road (1936) was the first Singleton-owned cinema to use that name. The frontage had a hint of Hollywood glamour, but the auditorium, located some way behind, was another brick and asbestos monster. (Tony Moss collection, CTA Archive)

Above: The Vogue in Langlands Road, Govan (1937) was the first of George Singleton's 'second generation' of cinemas designed by James McKissack. The tall curving frontage with vertical neon strips was very eye-catching. (Bruce Peter collection)

circuit to Oscar Deutsch's expansive Odeon empire, which was anxious to gain a Scottish foothold. Apart from the four modern super cinemas described above, the remainder of the Singleton circuit consisted of venerable halls – such as the Paragon in Glasgow's Gorbals (see above), converted from an abandoned church in the early days of cinema and subsequently little improved. Singleton later recalled that he only sent Deutsch photographs of his most recent cinemas and that Odeon paid well over the odds for the entire business, believing that all the cinemas were of a similar standard. Scruffy as some were, they were all good earners and at least Odeon gained Scottish representation in towns as far apart as Hawick, Dundee and Coatbridge as a result. Ironically, with the money he made from the Odeon deal, Singleton was able to build many more super cinemas. This later batch included some of McKissack's finest designs and each attempted to incorporate the bulk of its auditorium into a single, coherent architectural statement.

The Singleton-owned **Vogue** in Govan (1937) stood on a corner with a curving cream frontage in fluted tiles carried to full height and screening the mass of the auditorium, which was otherwise shielded from view by surrounding tenements. Smith & Welsh's **Riddrie** (1938) was located in the suburb of that name and developed the concept of differing volumes, arranged in proportion and building up to the centrally-placed name sign. The **Aldwych** in Cardonald (1939) was a gigantic rendered box tied tight by a deep cornice of a size and proportion to comprehend the auditorium within. All were big venues with between 2,000 and 2,500 seats.

James McKissack's final cinema design was also his firm's masterpiece. Opened in May 1939 as the city centre flagship of the Singleton circuit, the **Cosmo** was the largest and the only purpose-built 'art house' in Britain outside London's West End. By then McKissack's health was failing (he died in 1940), and so the Cosmo was actually drawn up by a younger assistant, W. J. Anderson. The idea for a Continental cinema came from Charles Oakley, a polymath Devonian who lectured at Glasgow University. Oakley was devoted to the city. He was a founder member of the Glasgow Film Society (formed in 1929 and thus having a claim to being the world's first) which specialised in screening the foreign films to which he

Above: The streamlined Riddrie cinema (James McKissack, 1938) when newly completed. (Bruce Peter collection)

Top right: The Aldwych at Cardonald (James McKissack, 1938) shows a more severely rectilinear design approach.

(Glasgow City Archives)

Left: The proscenium in the Cosmo cinema (James McKissack, 1939) with appliqué curtains and a clock featuring the signs of the zodiac.

(Bruce Peter collection)

Below: The Cosmo when newly completed. The geometric brick design shows Dutch influence.

(Bruce Peter collection)

The Cosmo's entrance foyer: cosmopolitanism asserts itself in the form of a globe above the stalls entrance. (Bruce Peter collection)

was so devoted. When 'talkies' came along the mainstream cinemas tended to show only English-language films, pushing out even the high-quality European ones. The Cosmo set out to put matters right. Moreover, while an independent cinema operator like Singleton could easily obtain sufficiently up-to-date British and American films to show in his big suburban cinemas, in the city centre there was greater competition and the 'first run' cinemas belonging to Paramount, Gaumont and ABC showed the newest releases. Thus, the Cosmo plugged a gap in the market where there was no direct competition. The name was derived from 'Cosmopolitan', a small cinema associated with Cambridge University, with which Oakley was familiar. Singleton, whose interest in the venture was more business-like, insisted that a catchy five-letter name was needed.

The Cosmo's geometric brown brick façade was clearly influenced by the **Curzon**, an upmarket art cinema in London built in 1934 and designed by Francis Lorne of Burnet, Tait & Lorne – a highly respected Glasgow firm which also had a substantial London office. The Curzon was a building of elegant simplicity. Its neatly-detailed brick frontage was partly the result of fierce opposition to a cinema opening in the heart of Mayfair and it had to be less than thirty-five feet high. The Curzon, in turn, was inspired by the work of Willem Dudok. As town architect of Hilversum in the Netherlands between 1920 and 1935, Dudok successfully solved the problem of creating visual integrity in large public buildings. His brick-clad structures were conceived as series of massed cubic volumes playing off each other and were often topped by a central tower feature. His designs were obvious models for cinema architects.

Standing on an awkward sloping site on Rose Street, near busy Sauchiehall Street, the Cosmo was similarly well-proportioned. Clad in Ayrshire brick finished with faience cornices, detailed in cream and amber, and set on a base of black Swedish granite, the cinema's façade was as much an expression of internationalism as its programmes. As planners insisted that the Cosmo should be set back from the adjacent frontages, a disproportionately large canopy and sign were fitted to advertise its presence. The international theme was continued inside, where the two-storey-high foyer had a globe over the stalls entrance. The vestibule was panelled

in walnut. Two suites of offices, including a directors' room, were provided. The neutral and pink-toned walls of the streamlined, 850 seat auditorium flowed in a series of subtle curves towards the proscenium and, together with satin curtains and indirect, delicately coloured lighting, created the desired air of sophistication. 'Entertainment for the Discriminating' was its trademark.

Charles Oakley based his programming on that of the Academy cinema in Oxford Street, London, which was regarded as the best art film house in Britain. Despite his intellectualism, Oakley was passionate about cartoons, and these were regularly shown at the Cosmo. He would sometimes telephone round the Glasgow cinemas to find where one was playing and, while Cosmo audiences enjoyed a highbrow European movie, he would go off to revel in animated magic at a rival cinema! Quality European films, particularly French ones, were to feature centrally in Cosmo programmes throughout its career, the only exception being during the war years when revivals and run-of-the-mill commercial attractions were shown.

In 1974 the Cosmo was bought by the Scottish Film Council to become the **Glasgow Film Theatre.** It was subdivided into a 404 seat cinema in the former balcony and a conference-cum-exhibition space in the stalls. In 1988, a 144 seat cinema replaced the conference room and later a bar (now known as Café Cosmo) was added. The Glasgow Film Theatre is now independently owned and makes a significant and unique contribution to the cultural life of Glasgow and the West Coast of Scotland.

James McKissack's great rival in cinema design was the firm of Charles J. McNair & Elder, also based in Glasgow. Since designing his first cinema, Scott's Electric Theatre, in 1911, McNair had inevitably gathered his own group of clients whose cinemas often competed directly with those designed by McKissack. Working closely with George Urie Scott's Cinema Construction Company, which built all the cinemas his office designed, McNair & Elder became the most productive architects of Scottish super cinemas. Working with them was a young assistant, Robert Forsyth:

'McNair was a genial wee man – very good with clients. Scott would come into the office with large-scale maps of districts around Glasgow. He'd have selected suitable sites for building cinemas and drawn

The Regal, Stirling (McNair & Elder, 1932) – one of a series of large cinemas designed for ABC in Scottish provincial towns.
(Bruce Peter collection)

The Regal Coatbridge, 1950s (McNair & Elder, 1936) behind the right of the Coatbridge Fountain. (Bruce Peter collection)
Below: The Plaza, Govan (McNair & Elder, 1936) shows streamlining elements applied to the entrance area, but a large shed containing the auditorium behind. (Glasgow City Archives)

The Regal, Falkirk (McNair & Elder, 1934) – a partial re-build of the Grand Theatre by which means the theatre's side wall became the cinema's main frontage. (Bruce Peter collection)

Left: The 1938 Empire Exhibition was held in Glasgow's Bellahouston Park and was an attempt to boost the city's struggling economy. In the background, the Tower of Empire by Thomas Tait can be seen. The foreground is dominated by the bandstand designed by the noted architectural acoustics pioneer, Hope Bagenal. (Bruce Peter collection)

Below: A general view of the Empire Exhibition, featuring the ICI Pavilion by Basil Spence on the left and the pavilion of British Railways by Joseph Emberton to the right. Beyond is the Palace of Engineering by Tait, the composition of which should be compared with the Ascot cinema, illustrated on page 108. (Bruce Peter collection)

concentric rings around them to find out how many people were living within a one-, two-, three-mile radius and he'd know how many tram routes there were passing by and what the frequency of service was. Robert Elder, who became a partner in the early-1930s, did most of the designing. Elder was a bachelor who was pretty much married to his drawing board. A man of few words, he sat quietly chain-smoking as he drew up the projects, which he then handed to me or one of the other assistants to detail.'

McNair & Elder designed for Scott's own companies, for the prominent A.B. King Circuit and, most importantly, for Maxwell's powerful and expansive ABC circuit all over Scotland. Following on from the 'semi-atmospheric' designs in Riddrie and Hamilton (see above), McNair & Elder next produced **Regal** cinemas at Stirling (1932) and Falkirk (1934). Externally, these were unattractive buildings, but they were very strongly constructed and had interiors in the 'jazz moderne' manner. The **Regal**, Coatbridge, the **Plaza**, Govan and the **Princes**, Springburn were all completed in 1936. Externally, these showed little improvement over the earlier projects, but all had impressive streamlined interiors, which McNair & Elder became particularly adept at designing. Typically, they were comfortable but solidly constructed buildings, which used hard-wearing materials designed for punishing use. To take an example, the commodious 1,958 seater Coatbridge Regal had spacious foyers with brightly coloured terrazzo floors. There were twin pay boxes in the foyer and crush halls which could accommodate hundreds, a considerable asset on cold and wet winter nights. The auditorium walls curved gently towards the proscenium with the balcony front curving in parallel (creating a perfectly oval void between the balcony and screen). To either side, horizontal slits with decorative grillwork both ventilated the space and focused attention on the screen. Above, deep cornices concealed colour-change lighting, made by Holophane, which suffused the walls and ceiling in slowly changing colours. According to Robert Forsyth:

'Having erected the steel frames, the roof would be fitted, then teams of Irish brickies would come on site to build the outside walls. While this was happening, the balcony cantilevers would be assembled. Its main girder was always the heaviest piece of structure and

one of the first items to arrive on site right at the beginning of construction. Next, while the floors were being laid, wooden batons would be attached to the steelwork onto which expanded metal sheeting was fixed. Specialist plasterers sprayed this with layer upon layer of plaster to make the domed ceiling, which was the best shape for acoustic reasons. The rest of the auditorium would then be lined in plasterboard, which was also sprayed with a skin of coarse plaster to lessen the reverberation. Pegboard tiles were fitted to the rear walls to further dampen this. All the construction work was co-ordinated with the Cinema Construction Company, with whom we had a very close relationship to make sure that the work progressed as smoothly and efficiently as possible because designing and building a cinema was a complex art. Incidentally, these ABC projects were slightly unusual in that they had a barrier across the stalls to keep the cheaper 'front' strictly separate from the more expensive 'rear.' This was supposed to prevent customers from moving in the dark to the better seats, but the arrangement probably cost more to staff than it ever saved in lost ticket revenue.'

Later McNair & Elder projects for George Urie Scott himself and for A.B. King had much more inspired exteriors as well. The **State** cinema in King's Park (1937), which stood at the crest of a hill, was particularly

The Empire cinema at the Empire Exhibition, designed by Alister G. MacDonald. (Bruce Peter collection)

The State cinema, King's Park, Glasgow (McNair & Elder, 1937). (Glasgow City Archives)

The streamlined interior of the State when latterly in use as a bingo hall. (David Trevor-Jones)

The Lyceum, Govan (McNair & Elder, 1937) – perhaps the architects' most striking design and certainly one of the most unusual as the auditorium was located far to the rear of the frontage, which was actually a free-standing screening wall. (Glasgow City Archives)

The Lyceum's circular entrance foyer and island pay box. (Bruce Peter collection)

The Lyceum's spacious auditorium; at the time of writing, this remains intact but in semi-derelict condition. (Bruce Peter collection)

impressive with the receding volumes of the foyer spaces expressed in white render and the structure of the auditorium exposed in darker horizontal bands and held within a low white rendered wall with vertical fins. It was one of two cinemas built for Scott's Cathcart Picture Playhouse Company – the other was the **State**, Shettleston. The reason for this, Forsyth remembers, was that McNair & Elder had found a new design imperative:

'It was the Empire Exhibition which really put the frighteners under architects up here [in Glasgow]. Previously, we had been aware of what was happening on the Continent as the architecture magazines were full of white projects with flat roofs, but they somehow seemed remote. We kept saying "perhaps in a few years…" but, suddenly, there was Tait and his design for this great show right here on our doorstep, so we went modern almost overnight…'

McNair & Elder's best designs, however, were both for cinemas controlled by Alexander B. King. King's role in the development of cinema and film was seminal, not only as a major exhibitor but also as an organiser, lobbyist and diplomat, Born in 1888, he became involved in the entertainment business at the tender age of twelve. Every evening after he finished work with the Clyde Navigation Trust, he sold programmes at the Royal Princess' Theatre in the Gorbals. When the show was over he had to pick up the discarded programmes, dust them off and flatten them out for re-sale. It was a humble start for a man who was to achieve so much. King was politically and socially astute as well as energetic and as he worked his way upwards in cinema and film distribution management he made many useful connections in the Scottish business community. Between the wars, he was responsible for booking films for many of Scotland's independent cinemas. A shrewd negotiator, he often sent unco-operative film renters away from his office quite belittled by his knack of paring their charges to the bone. He sat on the boards of several cinema circuits – including Caledonian Associated Cinemas – and he was a member of the General Council of the Cinema Exhibitors Association, chairing their Entertainments Tax Committee. In the 1935 Budget, this Committee was instrumental in securing a remission in Entertainment Tax for cinema seats costing up to 6d, a great relief to the small independent exhibitors whom King supported so enthusiastically.

Later on, King served as Film Officer for Scotland at the Ministry of Information during the years when it looked as though a Scottish film-making industry might take off. In 1937 he was made a Deputy Lieutenant of the City of Glasgow and was awarded the CBE. Another accolade came in 1944 when he was knighted in recognition of his wartime activities with the Ministry of Information and his support for charitable causes which helped the war effort. King was a man of vision and influence throughout his long career. In the fifties, as vice-chairman of the Scottish Tourist Board (which he remained until his death in 1973), he supervised the world-wide distribution of documentary films about Scotland and, in 1960, he founded Grampian Television, whose chairman he was for eight years.

When the **Lyceum** in Govan, a former theatre, burned down, King commissioned McNair & Elder to design a suitable replacement. The old theatre had followed the line of the neighbouring tenements but, as there was insufficient space for the planned 2,600 seater replacement, this was located at right-angles further behind. The new building was therefore distinguished by a three-storey-high curtain wall frontage which swept around a large corner site in a graceful curve, but had open space directly behind it. Above the five doorways and canopy were what appeared to be five tall recessed windows with back-lit glass blocks, separated by soaring blue tiled mullions. The rest was clad in tiles and facing brick and the flowing lines were emphasised by a narrow black cornice. There were prominent display panels, carefully placed to be in line with the top deck windows of passing tramcars. The foyer spaces were lofty and circular with coloured terrazzo floors radiating from the middle and there was a matching 'island' pay box. A greater contrast with the sooty ashlar tenements next door would have been difficult to imagine.

McNair & Elder's final cinema project was also the one which most obviously owed the origins of its design to the Empire Exhibition. The **Ascot** (1939) was almost identical in form and layout to the Palace of Engineering at the Exhibition. Built for Great Western Cinemas, a company in which Alexander B. King was involved, its name allegedly was chosen as a result of its being partly financed by a winning bet by another of its directors. Five tall windows, with slim fins between, were recessed in the massive cream tiled frontage with flanking drum-

Above: The Ascot at Anniesland in Glasgow (McNair & Elder, 1939) undergoing light maintenance shortly after the Second World War. The building closely resembled the Palace of Engineering at the Empire Exhibition. (Bruce Peter collection)

Bottom left: The cinema magnate Sir A.B. King – a director of the Ascot and numerous other Scottish cinemas. (Bruce Peter collection)

Bottom right: The Ascot's curvaceous auditorium, photographed after closure as a bingo club and shortly before demolition for a development of flats. Only the frontage was retained. (Bruce Peter)

Right: The foyer of the Edinburgh Regal (W.R. Glen, 1938). ABC favoured twin pay boxes to speed up the flow of patrons. (Bruce Peter collection)

Below: The Regal's entrance in Lothian Road in the 1950s. The cinema was integrated into a larger office and retail development.

(Bruce Peter collection)

Below: The Regal's splendid streamlined auditorium, viewed from the front stalls and showing the decorative grillwork, a feature of many Glen-designed cinemas.

(Bruce Peter collection)

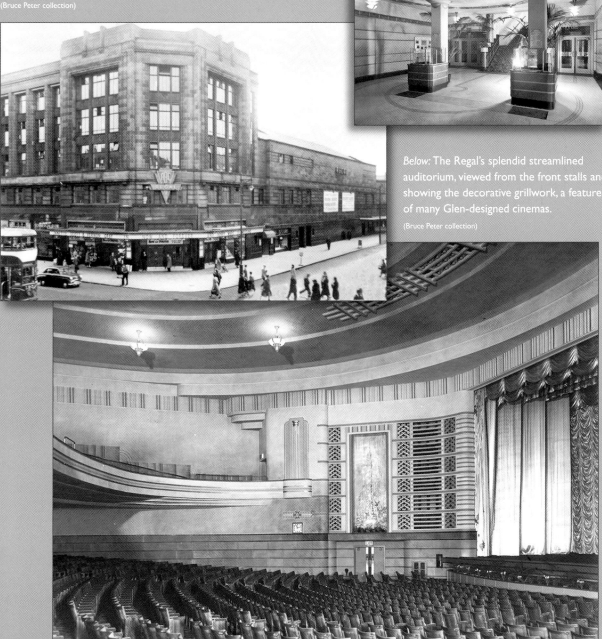

Above left: The Regal's café with rattan furniture – rather like a 1930s ocean liner winter garden. (Bruce Peter collection)

Above right: The interior of the Regal, Arbroath (W.R. Glen, 1940). (Bruce Peter collection)

The Odeon in Hamilton (Thomas Braddock and Andrew Mather, 1938). (Bruce Peter collection)

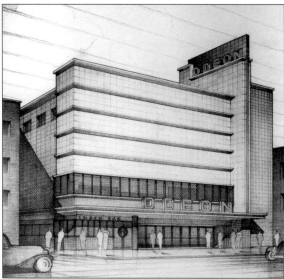

Another un-built Odeon, this time planned for Dumbarton.
(Bruce Peter collection)

The Odeon in Motherwell, also by Braddock and Mather and opened in 1938. (Bruce Peter collection)

Above: The Odeon in Ayr (1938), facing Burns Statue Square, was a slightly more ambitious design from Mather's office.
(Bruce Peter collection)

Left: A rendering of an un-built design by Keith Roberts for an Odeon at Partick in Glasgow. (Bruce Peter collection)

Below: A convincing imitation of the Odeon style, La Scala in Clydebank (Lennox D. Paterson, 1938) actually ended up as a member of the ABC circuit. (Bruce Peter collection)

shaped volumes containing the stairs to the balcony. The war, and materials rationing, started during construction, and so special permission was needed to complete it to an amended design. The roof, specially strengthened with extra trusses, was supposedly blast-proof.

Although McNair & Elder designed almost all of the new Scottish ABC cinemas in the early- and mid-1930s, towards the end of the decade a few were produced by ABC's London-based house architect, W.R. Glen. Photographs of Glen at the height of his powers in the 1930s show a stylish man who was reputedly a snappy dresser, wearing sharply-cut double-breasted suits and white spats over his shoes. His daughter, Gari Todd, recalls that he was 'very proper, very gentlemanly, liked us to speak, dress and behave nicely….and, so far as we could judge, was very formal in dealings with others.' While it is risky to assess an architect by family memories, this assessment rings true when looking at the qualities of his considerable output.

By the mid-1930s, Glen was in his stride and his fully-fledged ABC 'house style' was emerging. During the decade, he designed seventy-plus cinema projects, mainly in towns and cities throughout England. He became particularly adept at handling foyer spaces, usually making them airy double-height volumes. These were lit by chrome pendant light fittings and the walls were often adorned with medallions and friezes in low relief. There were generally twin pay boxes set well back in the foyer and grand staircases to either side to the circle, which typically curved round to meet an open landing bridge in the middle, with a decorative metal balustrade. Another set of stairs between the pay boxes led down to the stalls crush hall, because Glen cinemas were either excavated to below ground level or made good use of naturally sloping sites to keep the stalls low. Unlike 'super' cinemas by other architects, which had tortuous stairways and tunnel-like passages, in Glen designs the audiences made a straightforward progress to their seats. Glen was fortunate that ABC always sought a strong presence in the high street, rarely accepting sites that allowed only narrow approaches and usually buying sufficient ground to set the auditorium block some way back. This gave him the space to create tall entrance areas, whereas in the vast majority of other cinemas the main foyer was more compressed with lower ceilings to use the space above for facilities such as a circle lounge, a café, ballroom or offices.

A characteristic Glen auditorium would be tall with conspicuous decorative grillwork and a boldly modelled ceiling with dramatically sculpted ribs, illuminated troughs and scalloped edges picked out in gold, stepping down towards the screen opening. The front emergency exits from the circle would face backwards with short slips and the auditorium would therefore narrow in front of the circle and taper further inwards towards the screen. According to the cinema historian, Allen Eyles, 'John Maxwell was a shrewd taskmaster and even when Glen submitted a plan to his exact specification and costing, Maxwell would demand that a thousand pounds or so be lopped off the final estimate and this was generally achieved.' Consequently, the majority of Glen exteriors were less demonstrative than rival cinemas, yet most had a civic dignity and they were carefully fitted into the townscape. Though no two cinemas from Glen's office were the same, they had in common ingenious planning and the skilful manipulation of space.

The **Regal**, Edinburgh (1939) typified this as it was incorporated into Lion House, an office and retail development on Lothian Road by Stewart, Kaye & Walls. Only the canopy and entrance doors distinguished the Regal externally. Its interior represented Glen at his best with the auditorium gracefully streamlined with striking ventilation grilles to either side of the screen opening and illuminated silk panels depicting Pierrot and Harlequin. For an ABC cinema, it was large with 2,769 seats and a café.

The **Palace** in Arbroath (1940) replaced an older cinema of the same name (one of ABC's idiosyncrasies was that it always retained names when it replaced existing cinemas with new 'supers'). This cinema was more angular than the lavish Edinburgh Regal, perhaps reflecting its cramped site tucked up a side street and also no doubt a much tighter budget. Certainly, it had a most unimaginative plain brick exterior. W.R. Glen designed one further Scottish cinema before the Second World War – the **Regal** in Aberdeen, but the war halted construction and it remained a partially-completed shell until permission was given for it finally to be completed in 1955, but by another architect (see below).

The film world in Britain was shocked when John Maxwell died in October 1940, aged 63. Apart from the film studios, his most important legacy was the ABC chain with its cinemas in every city and town of note. Having passed through a number of asset-stripping owners, it existed until recently, but in a much reduced form.

After taking over a chain of rather basic, although very profitable, cinemas when he purchased the original Singleton circuit in 1936, Odeon's hard-working founder, Oscar Deutsch, began a new building programme to get a bigger share of the lucrative Scottish market. In 1938 his London architect, Andrew Mather, was commissioned to design three new **Odeons** at Hamilton, Motherwell and Ayr. These were reputedly the work of one of Mather's assistants, Thomas Braddock, and they certainly compared poorly with cinemas of the same size and vintage by Scottish firms. All three were at first entirely clad in cream faience tiles, but these soon began to fall off and were replaced by cement render. The first to open was at Ayr, located on a prominent site facing onto Burns Statue Square and next to the railway station, and it is the only survivor today. Deutsch next proposed a number of much larger Odeons to be developed, mainly around Glasgow. Another Mather assistant, Keith Roberts, drew up schemes for Odeons at Bridgeton, Partick, Townhead, Dumbarton and Falkirk. None was built due to financial difficulties and materials shortages caused by the worsening political situation in Europe, but Roberts' scheme for Partick evidently would have been a particularly impressive building.

La Scala in Clydebank (1938) emulated the best English Odeons – such as those at Harrogate and Sutton Coldfield by Cecil Clavering – which were, at least, an excellent source of inspiration. It was a conspicuous building to seat 2,648, prominently sited on a hillside and with a soaring advertising tower. Designed by Lennox D. Paterson of Hamilton for a company chaired by Alexander B. King, La Scala was luxurious with nautical decoration inspired by Cunard's liner *Queen Mary*, then only recently completed at John Brown's nearby shipyard. The screen curtains originally had the soaring bows of the two Cunard 'Queens' pointing in from each side. For an entertainment-hungry public, the ocean liner represented glamour, escapism and modernity – it was only a short step for the actual motifs of these vessels to be transferred directly to buildings. The *Queen Mary* had caught the public imagination as holder of the Blue Riband for the fastest Atlantic crossing and was the pride of Britain's Merchant Navy, representing a great economic and technical achievement. Clydebank's finest cinema miraculously survived the blitz unscathed and was sold to ABC in 1959 to replace its fire-damaged Empire. Today it is vacant, having previously been internally subdivided for snooker and bingo and externally mutilated by having its tower and canopy removed. What was once a stylish landmark is now a derelict eyesore.

It would, however, be disingenuous to pretend that all Scottish cinemas built in the 1930s were of the quality of those described above – far from it. Some were inexpensively converted from Edwardian premises by using as much of these existing structures as possible. For example, the **Wishaw Picture House**, which had first opened back in 1913, was reconstructed in the summer of 1938, a time when business was slacker. First, the frontage was dismantled and Corrie & Millar of Wishaw erected a new tiled elevation with a tower and fluting, all outlined at night in red and blue neon. The following summer, the auditorium was modernised. In Greenock, the **BB Cinema**, which stood at the corner of Argyle Street and dated from 1914, was re-built in 1935 with a more modern frontage, designed by the Glasgow-based architect, J. Hamilton Neil, although its ornate interior remained unaltered. (Incidentally, it had nothing to do with the well-known BB Cinema circuit of J.J. Bennell. Instead, it was developed by a local company, Greenock BB Cinema Ltd.)

In 1936 A.E. Pickard had the Norwood ballroom in St George's Road, Glasgow converted into the **Norwood** cinema. Its structure consisted of an asbestos roof, supported on either side by existing buildings. True to form, its original promoter had devised an outlandish frontage topped with two replica cantilevers of the Forth Railway Bridge, a clock suspended between them and a big plywood replica of the Cunard liner *Queen Mary* sailing underneath as a Bassett-Lowke model locomotive crossed the Bridge! Hard though it is to imagine, the interior was even more curious with a display case containing a Kilmarnock edition of Burns poetry marked as 'A Gift for Whichever Leader Wins the War' in the foyer. The stadium style of auditorium was clad in faceted mirrors of different colours – no wonder it was known as 'Pickard's Crystal Palace'. The reflections caused by the mirrors must have made watching a film at the Norwood very difficult.

Left and above: To compete with super cinemas, many older premises were modernised and enlarged. The BB Cinema in Greenock (1914) was reconstructed in 1935.

(Bruce Peter collection and Tony Moss, CTA Archive)

The Picture House in Wishaw dated from 1913 and was substantially re-built in 1938 with a new tiled frontage. (Bruce Peter collection)

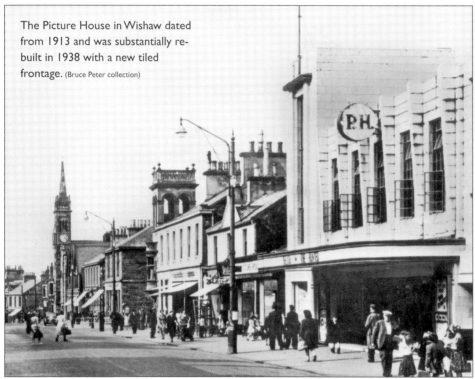

Left: A sketch of Pickard's Norwood cinema, St George's Road, Glasgow, as completed in 1936. (Bruce Peter collection)
Below: A post-war view of the Norwood, shortly after it joined the ABC circuit and minus the *Queen Mary* replica.

(Bruce Peter collection)

A post-war view of the Birks cinema in Dunkeld Street, Aberfeldy (1939). (Bruce Peter collection)

The auditorium of the Rex in Newmilns, Ayrshire (Lennox & McMath, 1939). (Bruce Peter collection)

A 'dreich' day in Denny in the late-1930s with the new Cinema De Luxe providing a striking contrast with the existing townscape. (Bruce Peter collection)

The tiny Picture House in Ballater, seen in the 1950s. (Bruce Peter collection)

The 800 seater Tinto in Forth & Wilsontown. Such cinemas served wide farming hinterlands. (Bruce Peter collection)

Small Town Wonders

IN the 1930s, Scotland was movie-mad, and so even communities as small as Newport-on-Tay (the **Rio**), Anstruther (the **Empire** and the **Regal**), Grantown-on-Spey (the **Picture House**), Ballater (the **New Cinema**) and Newmilns (the **Rex**) could sustain a local cinema. Some, such as the **Picture House** in Newton Stewart, a 600 seater in a village of only 1,914 residents, catered to expansive farming hinterlands. The 800 seater **Tinto** cinema in Forth and Wilsontown was named after a nearby mountain in the Southern Uplands, to serve a small mining village of 1,615 residents, giving a ratio of one cinema seat to every two villagers! Fraser Stewart of Glasgow designed it for a flamboyant showman called Mickey Burns. When mining declined, the Tinto quickly became a white elephant and its inevitable closure followed in 1966.

Next, Burns developed the **Windsor** in Carluke (1937) and fitted it out with interiors rescued from the famous Cunard liner *Mauretania* which had been scrapped at Inverkeithing on the Forth. The Windsor's brick exterior represented a Moorish fortress of sorts with defensive walls, battlements and a gatehouse, topped by one of the glazed domes from the *Mauretania*'s Winter Garden. The foyer had panelling from *Mauretania*'s social hall and more ship timbers were used as dados in the 1,300 seat auditorium. Shortly after it opened, Burns' cinemas were sold to the Gourock Picture House Company after a dispute with a film renter who accused him of fiddling the box office takings. Burns went to the 20th Century-Fox office in Glasgow and remonstrated with the renter. Although he maintained his innocence and faced no legal action, all the major distributors barred him from receiving films. Film renters enjoyed a strong position in the 1930s

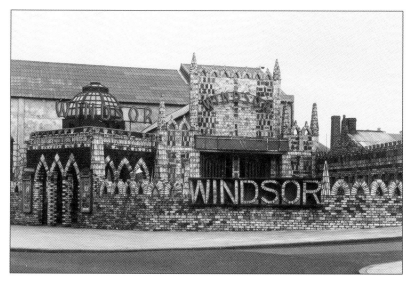

Above left: The outlandish frontage of the Windsor in Carluke (1937) with a lantern from the Cunard liner *Mauretania*'s winter garden atop the gatehouse. (Bruce Peter collection)

Above right: The Windsor's auditorium. (Bruce Peter collection)

Bottom right: The Windsor's foyer, featuring more fixtures and fittings from the *Mauretania*'s interior. (Bruce Peter collection)

Above: Staff pose on the front steps of the newly completed Rex in Stonehouse (1937). (Bruce Peter collection)

Right: The Rex's entrance hall; the ceiling panels, lighting and possibly the doors are all from the scrapped liner *Homeric*. (Bruce Peter collection)

Below: The auditorium uses the ceiling of the *Homeric*'s First Class dining saloon, while the side walls are assembled from ceiling panels from other areas of the liner. The result is very convincing as a luxury cinema and demonstrates how ingenious showmen were. (Bruce Peter collection)

to dictate terms to smaller operators such as Burns, whether fair or otherwise. The Windsor went over to bingo in the 1960s but latterly fell into disuse. The derelict building was demolished in 1987; however, Burns' house, which was in the same style, survives.

Although its exterior dated from 1937, the history of the **Rex** in Stonehouse, a small Lanarkshire village, can be traced back to 1913 when the shipping line North German Lloyd ordered the Atlantic liner *Columbus* from the Schichau Unterweser shipyard at Danzig. The First World War intervened and the vessel was completed as a war reparation for the British White Star Line as *Homeric* (to replace *Britannic*, a sister of the infamous *Titanic*, which was sunk by enemy action in the Mediterranean). She was not a success, being too small and slow and was sent for scrap at Inverkeithing in 1936. John Sheeran, a travelling showman, found some chandeliers from the liner in a Kirkcaldy flea market. He quickly made for the scrap-yard where he bought the entire First Class dining saloon to decorate the interior of the Rex, then under construction. Sheeran's architect baulked at the prospect of trying to fit a liner interior (with built-in sheer and camber) into a cinema auditorium, and so he resigned from the job, leaving the showmen to complete it on their own. The ornate mahogany panels were brought to Stonehouse by

train and re-assembled in the 750 seat auditorium. The result was impressive and when Sir Harry Lauder opened the Rex on 22 January 1937, it was hailed as 'Lanarkshire's King of Picture Houses.' Jack Buchanan commented, when visiting to promote a film, that the last time he'd seen 'that ceiling', he'd been eating dinner half way across the Atlantic! Business was brisk before the war but, when many villagers were conscripted away for war service, attendance declined severely. The Rex closed in the mid-1960s and, since re-faced, has become a warehouse for the Sheerans amusement machines. The unique interior is still intact.

Market towns were lucrative places in which to develop a cinema as they were at route centres and could therefore easily be accessed by thinly-spread rural populations. For many farm workers, going to the pictures was a treat on market day. To enable their development, local businessmen – neighbouring shop owners, lawyers and even haulage contractors – would collaborate with a cinema magnate (usually Alexander B. King) for expertise and a good supply of films. Typically, such projects would be financed by a combination of their own investment, a share issue and, if necessary, a bank loan. These locally-owned cinemas were hailed as important civic amenities and they offered many patrons the unaccustomed luxuries of fitted carpets, concealed colour-change interior lighting and several sets of embroidered and festooned curtains over the screen. The romance of the movies affected every aspect of their design and operation.

The **Regal** in Lanark, a large and well-appointed 1,316 seater with a café, was financed in this way. As an important market town in the Clyde Valley, Lanark served a large hinterland and the Regal was always a prosperous cinema. The building was designed by Lennox D. Paterson of Hamilton for a local syndicate in which Alexander B. King was a key shareholder. Lord Dunglass opened the cinema on 31 August 1936 when

The Regal in Lanark (Lennox D. Paterson, 1936), decorated for Lanimer Day in the early-1950s.

(Bruce Peter collection)

Above left: The café in the Regal, Lanark with typical rattan furniture, Art Deco carpeting and portraits of screen stars adorning the walls. (Bruce Peter collection)

Above right: The Lanark Regal's auditorium in latter-day use as a bingo hall in the mid-1990s. The shovel-shaped ceiling lights and horizontal detailing around the proscenium are typical details of 1930s cinemas of this type. (Scott McCutcheon)

Charlie Chase in *Manhattan Monkey Business* and Laurel and Hardy in *The Bohemian Girl* were the big attractions.

In West Lothian, meanwhile, Lothians Star Theatres, belonging to Messrs Millar and Walker of Bathgate, was a small circuit which developed four impressively modern cinemas during the late-1930s to serve mining towns and villages in West Lothian and Lanarkshire. It should be remembered that some coal miners probably had a greater acquaintance with modern architecture than most in the 1930s as new pit-head baths frequently were striking examples of the idiom. Perhaps surprisingly, their architectural vocabulary had a clear affinity with cinemas of the period – many had towers for both practical (they were good places to put water tanks and plenum rooms) and symbolic reasons.

The **Regals** in West Calder (1937) and Shotts (1939) were the work of Dick Peddie and J.R. McKay and each had a tower feature in the 'Odeon' manner – from which cinema architects seem to have found constant inspiration. Those in Armadale (1937) and Bathgate (1938) were externally more conservative symmetrical designs by A.D. Haxton of Leven, but the latter was distinguished by a remarkable Art Deco interior design by John Alexander. Alexander was a Newcastle-based designer and fibrous plaster manufacturer who produced some of the most flamboyant British cinema interiors of the 1930s, mainly in his native North-East of England. Although he had devised colour schemes for Green's Playhouses in Glasgow and Dundee and supplied moulded plaster decorations for the latter (see above), so far as is known the Bathgate Regal was his only other Scottish work. The decorative scheme consisted of bas relief panels depicting nude Roman charioteers on either side of the screen. Evidently these caused outrage when the cinema was new as church congregations demanded that they be removed or, at least, 'made decent.' The three-dimensional plasterwork was incorporated into an intricate painted scheme on the side walls and ceiling, which has since been lost through repainting. Fortunately, the Regal survives in

The Regal in Shotts (Peddie & McKay, 1939) – another building providing a stark contrast with the 'couthy' sandstone buildings with which it is surrounded. (Bruce Peter collection)

Above left: The superbly restored Regal in Bathgate (A.D. Haxton, 1938) nowadays serves as a community theatre and venue for events. Its revival shows how, with some imagination and willpower, old cinemas can be converted to serve as useful public amenities. (Bruce Peter)

Above right: The Regal's remarkable Art Deco plasterwork by John Alexander depicts Roman charioteers. When the cinema was first opened, this imagery caused considerable consternation to the local Parish Council who considered it obscene. (Bruce Peter)

otherwise intact condition as a community theatre and has recently been substantially renovated. (A similar painted interior design by Alexander has been recovered at the Northwick cinema, Worcester and shows how striking the Regal's auditorium must have looked when first opened.)

In the 1930s, there was such a vast demand for cinema buildings that not all involved architects in their design. Stellmacs – a building contractor who specialised in throwing up almost identical cinemas cheaply and quickly – constructed the **Regal** in Dalry (1935). It was the most intriguing of a number of rather perfunctory schemes they produced, mainly in small Ayrshire communities. What distinguished the Regal was that its façade represented a face – the second-floor windows obviously were eyes and the doors teeth. Stellmacs designed further similar examples in Dalbeattie, Camelon (near Falkirk), Lesmahagow and New Cumnock, the latter being an enlargement of an earlier cinema.

The one in Lesmahagow belonged to the Palmers, a show family who had once travelled with a Cinematograph show. Following its success, they built **Palmer's**

Picture House, a very basic wooden cinema, in 1910. After several hair-raising fires, it was replaced by the **Ritz** in 1939. In the meantime, and with the backing of local businessmen, a rival, the **Glebe**, had opened in 1929. It was then cut-throat competition between the Ritz and the Glebe. A suspicious fire devastated the Ritz only a few weeks after opening. With war-time building restrictions, the resourceful Palmers had to find materials for repair from fellow showmen. Robert Palmer recalls how, a few weeks after re-opening, youthful customers, who were known to be related to the owners of the Glebe, set fire to a row of seats in the balcony but, as the replacement floor was solid teak, the only wood the owners could lay their hands on, the building was saved. The Ritz closed in the late-1960s and was later demolished.

The Regal in Dalry, one of a number constructed by the building contractors, Stellmacs. This one had a frontage resembling a face in the 'jazz moderne' manner.

(Bruce Peter collection)

The auditorium of the New Picture House in the mid-1990s. (Bruce Peter)

The New Picture House in St Andrews (Gillespie & Scott, 1930) was a rare example of a cinema designed in the local vernacular. It is seen here in the 1970s. (Bruce Peter collection)

The Imperial in Methil (Haxton & Watson, 1925), shortly before demolition in the mid-1990s, vaguely resembled a Scottish keep. (Adrian Whitewick)

The Ritz in Linlithgow was converted from the town's Victoria Hall. The original façade was remodelled in 1937 with the original towers truncated and the parapet finished with battlements. (Bruce Peter collection)

The astonishing Viking in Largs (1939) – one of a number of highly imaginative designs for entertainment buildings of various kinds by James Houston. (Bruce Peter collection)

The Radio in Kilbirnie (James Houston, 1937) celebrated radio broadcasting with a fake transmission tower and flashing neon zig-zags. (RCAHMS)

The Radio's auditorium as originally completed with murals on either side of the proscenium. When CinemaScope was installed in the 1950s, this was re-modelled, as shown on page 133. (RCAHMS)

As we have seen, cinema architects seemingly did everything to avoid referring in any way to Scottish architectural traditions. Cinemas were, after all, an escape from the monotony of small-town life. The port corchère of the **New Picture House** in St Andrews (1930) by the local architects, Gillespie & Scott, was a rare exception which did indeed attempt to reflect its surroundings by using locally-appropriate finishes and details, such as crow-stepped gables, pantiles and harling. Yet, it still became a landmark on North Street and a favourite haunt for generations of university students. Its commodious foyer, with plenty of space to wait for a seat in warmth and relative comfort, was a welcome blessing in St Andrews (which can be bitterly cold when the wind blows in from the North Sea). Today, it is one of Scotland's most intact surviving cinema buildings. Its dingy auditorium is a delight with many well-preserved period fittings – painted panels depicting Scottish castles (by a native artist, Aida Walker), the original illuminated clocks and even the mantles for its gas secondary lighting are still in place. Elsewhere, the **Ritz** in Linlithgow was converted from a public hall and gained an extravagant castellated façade when the building was heightened for cinema use, while the **Imperial** in Methil (now demolished) was a more modest interpretation of a Scottish keep.

In complete contrast, James Houston, a Kilbirnie architect, produced two of Scotland's most outlandish but memorable cinema designs. The **Radio**, located in his home town, was built in 1937 and, as with the somewhat better known Radio City Music Hall in New

York City, took the miracle of electronic communication as its theme. It had a low, curvaceous white frontage with red and silver stripes, chrome eagles' heads with wings at each corner and a mighty fake radio beacon soaring above the entrance with a flashing light and purple neon zig-zags to broadcast its presence to the neighbourhood. Bearing in mind that the Radio stood at a crossroads in a staid little Ayrshire village of sandstone terraces and villas, this design was more than a little audacious. The foyer had a terrazzo and mosaic floor, which continued the theme of radio waves, and the auditorium was adorned with sprayed-on murals.

The **Viking** at Largs (1939) took its inspiration from the Battle of Largs, where the Scots trounced Viking invaders in 1263. A fantasy fortress in red, white and blue, it stood in landscaped gardens with a replica of a Viking longboat projecting from the entrance. Patrons entered between buttressed walls beneath battlements and a portcullis, which advertised the cinema's programme, was shut over the doors for security at night. Houston had also designed the nearby Moorings Ballroom, which was an equally remarkable ship-like structure. Unfortunately, both these striking buildings, which were part of the resort's seaside magic for countless holidaymakers, have disappeared. The Viking closed on 4 August 1973 to be converted into a bottling warehouse, but was later demolished. Happily, the Radio in Kilbirnie has recently been restored as a community centre – an excellent (yet sadly all too rare) example of how historic cinema buildings can serve communities even today.

Cinemas were intended to be seen at night when their architectural infelicities were shrouded in darkness. In the 1930s, many were adorned with neon outlining and floodlights. Here, the New Bedford Cinema in Glasgow's Eglinton Street (Lennox & McMath, 1932) looks particularly enticing. (Gary Painter collection)

Centre left: Poole's Roxy in Edinburgh's Gorgie Road (1937) attracts large crowds. (Bruce Peter collection)

Above: The Regent cinema in Glasgow's Renfield Street in the latter-1930s. Neon always looked somewhat out of place on buildings with historicist façade designs, such as this.
(Bruce Peter collection)

Left: The Broadway in Dundee – a member of the J.B. Milne circuit – has neon outlining on its Art Deco-style pediment.
(George Millar)

Top left: The Plaza in Kilmarnock (McNair & Elder, 1940) was tucked up a side street, hence the large vertical name sign angled to attract attention. (Bruce Peter collection)

Top right: The splendid George in Bellshill (Lennox D. Peterson, 1951) was the flagship of the George Palmer circuit. It is seen here with the neon being tested prior to opening to the public (note that the poster frames are empty). (Bruce Peter collection)

Below: The Spanish-American styled Toledo at Muirend on Glasgow's South Side neon-lit in the mid-1930s. (Gary Painter collection)

Above: The Ascot at Anniesland in Glasgow, covered in wartime camouflage paint, is decorated to celebrate VE Day in 1945.

(Bruce Peter collection)

Below: In Bellshill, what eventually became the George cinema lay in incomplete condition throughout the war years. The brickwork suggests that the frontage was to have been of a different design from that to which it was completed.

(Bruce Peter collection)

Post-War Decline and Revival

ON 3 September 1939 the announcement came that Britain was at war. Immediately, cinemas closed their doors as a safety precaution as it was thought dangerous to have large numbers of people together in one building. However, the authorities changed their minds and on 15 September the cinemas opened their doors again to even greater audiences than they had had before. The usual course of events was that during an air raid a message would be flashed on the screen or the manager would make an announcement. The show then continued as normal with as many seated under the extra protection of the balcony as possible. Very few chose to leave, correctly believing that if they did so they would not be as safe as in the cinema if a bomb fell in the street.

When war was declared, an embargo was placed on all cinema and entertainment building construction. Even immediately before the war, few new cinema projects were begun as there was a shortage of steel and other building materials, caused by economic and political instability. It would be sixteen years before cinema construction could begin again. Some schemes were halted in their tracks, such as the **Regal** in Aberdeen which stood from that point on as an empty, roofless shell. Only the steelwork and some of the brick cladding for the **George** in Bellshill had been erected when the building embargo came into force, yet other schemes, such as the **Ascot** in Anniesland (see above) and the very large **Green's Playhouse** in Wishaw, Lanarkshire were completed. This fourth and last of Green's mighty Playhouses opened in December 1940, as usual to a John Fairweather design. This was surely one of the most unsympathetic cinemas ever built, however, with an ugly flank of plain brick running parallel to Kirk Road, brightened only by a colourful roof, tiled in stripes of red

and green. The interior was monumental, seating a staggering 2,982, and the entire space was finished in shades of gold. The tea-room had walnut panelling and throughout the carpets gave a fluorescent glow. After an unprecedented building boom, it was Scotland's last new cinema for over fourteen years.

The rise of the cinema from its origins late in the nineteenth century until the outbreak of the Second World War was on a scale unprecedented in the history of entertainment. Its fall was equally dramatic with many problems confronting the exhibitor in the years of decline. The war years saw an unparalleled increase in cinema admissions, the numbers rising steadily to finish 60 per cent higher in 1945 than at the opening of hostilities in 1939. Television had been off the air for the duration; negligible opposition in pre-war days, its inevitable development and expansion were delayed by nearly seven years, leaving the cinema dominant in the field of visual entertainment. The population, meanwhile, swelled in the run-up to the D-Day landings with hundreds of thousands of Allied troops who were of the right age to be the most avid audience. They and the rest of the country temporarily escaped from their uncertain future in the cinemas, which were open all day, seven days a week. As the war drew to a close, the cinema trade viewed the future with uneasy optimism. The rapid expansion of the 1930s was obviously over, but could the cinema maintain its pre-eminent position in the future? Fears were allayed when 1946 recorded the highest number of admissions in cinema history. After six years of war, and faced with the prospect of a long period of austerity and reconstruction, the country was still badly in need of entertainment.

This euphoria, however, was short-lived as the world

had changed in six years. The war had thrown together millions of men and women from widely differing backgrounds, taken them abroad and introduced them to new ideas and technology. On the home front, women had stepped into jobs vacated by men called up for war service. Consequently, people's outlooks had broadened and expectations had increased. As the population settled down and picked up the threads of peace-time existence, the cinema became of decreasing significance in the social life of the country. In 1947 admissions dropped, due in part to a severe winter followed by a hot summer. They rallied somewhat in 1948, then declined rapidly from 1949 onwards.

The war had cost Britain an estimated £250 billion and the country was heavily in debt. Four-and-a-half million homes had been destroyed or damaged by bombing, as had large amounts of industry and infrastructure. Half the labour force was engaged in war production. Britain's reliance on imported raw materials necessitated very early in the war a ban on virtually all new building, except for factories supplying the war effort. When, at the end of the war, raw materials began to become available again, the country's meagre finances would cover only the more important items, such as food and machine tools necessary to re-equip industry for peace-time production and an export drive to re-pay war debt.

The cinema industry was particularly hard hit. Classified as luxury buildings, cinemas were subjected to severe restrictions. By 1945, most cinemas were worn out. Firstly, the neon had been removed from their façades to conform with black-out regulations. Shrapnel blasts, or even water penetration due to lack of repairs followed by freezing, left their tiled façades pot-marked and chipped. Sometimes, they were painted with khaki camouflage to make them less prominent as in wartime their very bold appearance, once an asset, had become a liability. Within, furnishings and carpets were threadbare, paintwork was sullied with tobacco smoke and equipment held together by running repairs made by the projectionists. Even the many sets of curtains and complex lighting effects were abandoned due to shortages of electricity in many places. Much of their mystique vanished and windowless, brick sheds with asbestos roofs were often pretty much all that remained.

Money was, in any case, in short supply particularly for the smaller independent exhibitors. In its evidence to the Portal Committee in February 1949, the Cinema Exhibitors Association estimated that, after the running costs of a smaller cinema had been met, a margin of barely 9 per cent remained with which to meet the demands of depreciation of property, redecoration and provision of new equipment. Building costs had by then risen to two-and-a-half times their 1939 level, and cash set aside to cover maintenance had been rendered inadequate by the sharp rise in replacement costs. In the eyes of the trade, the heaviest burden was the iniquitous Entertainments Tax. In 1938, the level stood at 16 per cent on income, but this had risen steeply during the war to over 40 per cent. The tax was on a sliding scale, rising from ½d on a 9d ticket (5½ per cent) to a hefty 2s 4d on a 5s ticket (nearly 47 per cent). So from a 5 shilling (25p) ticket the exhibitor received only 2s 8d (13p), little more than the Government. It is hardly surprising that when J. Arthur Rank (who by then controlled over 600 cinemas comprising both the Gaumont-British and Odeon circuits) prophesied mass closures of cinemas in a speech to shareholders at the end of 1953, he laid the blame squarely on Entertainments Tax, a sentiment echoed by NATKE (National Association of Theatrical and Kine Employees) at the Trades Union Congress conference.

In the immediate post-war years it must have seemed to the cinema owner that events were conspiring to bring about his ruin. Worse still, a world shortage of dollars was threatening the economy and it was essential that the outflow of funds be restricted and limited to the purchase of essentials. The cinema trade expected that profits on foreign films would be frozen in this country, until such time as the economy would permit their transfer to the foreign studios. It was stunned when, in August 1947, the Government introduced an import duty amounting to 75 per cent of profits on all imported films. The American studios, which inevitably bore the brunt of these measures, retaliated by refusing to send any films to Britain until the duty was lifted. American films were by far the most popular with audiences and British studios, notably Rank, struggled to fill the gap. As finance was difficult to obtain, quality was sacrificed for quantity, which compounded the cinemas' decline. Many cinemas had to rely on re-issues of old films and by the time the duty was lifted in March 1948, it had very nearly ruined the British film industry.

The severity of building restrictions was such that architects, surveyors and builders calculated that over half their time was spent obtaining permits for the use of various materials. Until June 1948, no more than £10 could be spent on building maintenance without a permit. In June 1951, the Chancellor of the Exchequer placed a limit of £5,000 on new entertainment projects and the following year restricted licenses for new schemes to areas where cinemas had been blitzed or no others existed.

Notwithstanding these draconian restrictions, on 24 November 1951 a sumptuous new cinema, the **George** in Bellshill, opened to great acclaim and gave a welcome boost to the entire British cinema industry (in pre-war days, such a provincial cinema opening would hardly have rated a mention in the trade press). Its owner and developer was the redoubtable George Palmer, born in Govan in 1903. He went to Govan High School and later

Top left: The foyer of the George in Bellshill (Lennox D. Paterson, 1951). (Bruce Peter collection)

Centre left: Staff pose in the George's balcony foyer: the manager, Bill McGee, is in the middle and behind him is Mrs George Palmer. The projectionists are in the back row. (Bruce Peter collection)

Above right: The George's auditorium, viewed from the rear stalls: there were two sets of curtains, the outer house tabs being adorned with tropical fish. (Bruce Peter collection)

Left: The frontage of the George when nearly complete and shortly before opening to the public. (Bruce Peter collection)

to Glasgow Technical College, before joining the Fairfield Shipyard as an electrical engineer. He lived in a cinema-mad neighbourhood where as many as fifteen different picture houses then competed for business. In 1922 Palmer left his job at Fairfield's to manage a local picture house (possibly the **Govan Cinema** in Maxwell's ABC circuit). His enthusiastic promotion of films brought him to the attention of the CEA Scottish Branch with an award for showmanship. After a year, he was appointed general manager of the prestigious La Scala in Glasgow's Sauchiehall Street, an amazing achievement for a mere twenty-year-old. In 1925, he moved with his wife and young daughter, Madge, to Bellshill, becoming manager of the **Alhambra** on the town's Main Street. Notwithstanding its idyllic name, Bellshill was in fact a grim mining village with a population of 20,000 in its environs at the heart of the Lanarkshire coalfield. Opened in 1923 by a local syndicate including Mr Antonio Verrecchia, who ran the neighbouring ice cream parlour, the Alhambra had been struggling. Palmer set about winning audiences back from the rival Picture House by booking the best available films (during his brief spell at La Scala, he had made many useful acquaintances in the CEA and could often get new releases before the opposition). In March 1929, the Alhambra became the first cinema in Lanarkshire to fit talkie equipment (supplied by Western Electric) and Jolson's *The Jazz Singer* opened there immediately after its record-breaking Glasgow run at the Coliseum. After seven years as manager, Palmer became managing director of the Alhambra in March 1932.

In May 1937, Palmer acquired the Regal in Mossend, a linear mining village a couple of miles to the east of Bellshill. This was a conversion from the old Pavilion Theatre, dating from 1902 (see above). The following year, Palmer went on a CEA trip to London to view the new Odeon, Leicester Square. The Lanarkshire showman must have been impressed, for on his return he bought a partially-completed cinema next to Bellshill Academy to construct what he described to *The Bellshill Speaker* as 'Lanarkshire's answer to the London Odeon', but Palmer's ambitious project was abruptly halted when war was declared. Later, Palmer's Associated G.P. Cinemas (formed in 1946) expanded all over the Central Belt of Scotland. Its two directors were George Palmer and his second wife, Janet, reputedly a formidable lady, who was the driving force behind the firm's continued expansion.

After much lobbying of the Attlee Government by the all-powerful National Union of Mineworkers Lanarkshire Branch, the building permits were finally granted in 1948, although materials shortages delayed completion by several more years. 'Lanarkshire's Wonder Cinema', according to *The Bellshill Speaker*, finally opened on 24 November 1951. For Palmer, this was a triumph; the first brand-new post-war picture-house anywhere in Britain and one of such high quality as to compete favourably with most city centre venues. The *Ideal Kinema* hailed it as 'Scotland's Contribution to Kinema Loveliness' and 'a Triumph of Beauty and Comfort'. Lennox D. Paterson had designed the George, and its exterior, clad entirely in cream, biscuit and black tiles with an internally-lit tower of glass blockwork at one end, was a startling addition to the grimy streets of Bellshill. The frontage was outlined in pink, red and blue neon with sixteen banks of scintillating white tubes under the canopy.

The interior was equally striking. The entrance doors, without frames, formed a continuous expanse of armour-plated glass to allow light to flood out into the street. There was a green and cream terrazzo floor with large 'GP' logos in mosaic and three concealed lights above. The circle foyer was panelled in walnut with an etched glass mirror frieze depicting local industries and transport in 'Festival of Britain' style. The auditorium walls were shaded in pink with intricate back-lit grilles, sprayed in silver, to either side of the screen and long troughs of cove lighting. The screen curtains were a memorable feature for there were three sets. First, the lights dimmed from the rear to the front and the grilles darkened. Then the vivid turquoise and green house tabs, with their colourful tropical fish, opened to the sides. Below, there were crimson velvet tabs with silver sequins. Once these slowly parted, a silver silk reefer tab scrunched up to reveal a vast screen. Cinema owners certainly knew about presentation in those days! The dark red carpet had interlocking leaves with the 'GP' motif and there was luxurious seating for 1,750. Hugh Quinn was assistant projectionist at the George from its opening:

'In the days running up to the opening, Mr and Mrs Palmer arrived first thing in the morning in their Rolls Royce, straight from home in Uddingston, to supervise the preparations. Bill McGee, one of Mr Palmer's longest-serving employees, was manager, and as the days went past, excitement grew. One

Top left: The foyer of the Plaza in Port Glasgow (Lennox & McMath, 1952) shows typical 1930s design detailing. (Bruce Peter collection)

Top right: The auditorium of the Plaza – again very typical of a super cinema of the late-1930s, which was when the building was actually designed. (Bruce Peter collection)

Centre left: The auditorium of the Regal, Aberdeen (C.J. Foster, 1954) with 'Festival of Britain' detailing – note the regular patterns of lights on the side walls and 'atomic' patterns around the proscenium. (Bruce Peter collection)

Right: The Union Street entrance of the Regal was beneath an existing tenement to which a vertical name sign was attached, the lettering being in a 'Festival of Britain' typeface.

(Bruce Peter collection)

During the 1950s, J.B. Milne of Dundee created a large circuit of provincial cinemas. This is his Regal in Blairgowrie (1938). (Bruce Peter collection)

La Scala in Cupar was converted from a United Presbyterian church in 1920. (George Millar)

The Regal in Auchterarder survived until recently as a furniture warehouse. Here, it is seen in its 1950s heyday. (George Millar)

The Picture House in Tayport (1911) was a basic shed but Milne had a streamlined name sign mounted on the front, as shown here. He invested generously to upgrade the cinemas he took over. (George Millar)

The interior of the Picture House in Tayport showing the typical bright screen tabs and decoration which typified Milne's cinemas. (George Millar)

night, they tested the neon lights outside, which brought all the kids in the area out to watch. There was a special, fully illustrated opening programme with a silver cover, which was an achievement in itself as materials rationing was still in force… On the opening night, Mrs Palmer was to have performed the opening, but she couldn't get the champagne bottle to break. Mr McGee tried smashing it on the door handles, but the audience just wanted to get inside because it was a freezing night. There was a grand reception upstairs with all the local councillors and everybody involved in building and equipping the cinema. The first film shown was a musical called *The Toast of New Orleans*…'

John Duddy, then a projectionist at the Rialto in Airdrie, was impressed by the standards set by the George:

'The George was the first cinema in Lanarkshire with CinemaScope and the only independent with four-track stereo sound. The team of projectionists gave a flawless performance on the 'Mircale Mirror' screen, which was supposed to show the new wide process to best advantage; it didn't as there were obvious joins in the panels, but the point was that the owners spared no expense in getting the best. Sometimes, I was told, magnetic stereo prints were flown to Glasgow at Mr Palmer's expense. It was no mean feat for a family-run cinema and a great stunt which none of its rivals ever attempted.'

For other cinema operators, it was not until 1954 that the announcement of a general relaxation of restrictions opened the way to any large-scale building. In Port Glasgow, Alex King had set up a company to develop a 'super' cinema back in 1939. It was to have been named the Eclipse. Lennox & McMath, who designed several large Glasgow cinemas, drew up plans but while construction was in progress, the war intruded. The empty shell lay untouched until 1952, when it was finally completed as the **Plaza**. In their haste to open the cinema, its owners saw no need to update their design to take new thinking into account. For sure, the Plaza was very well-appointed, but in typical 'thirties' style – the Festival of Britain might never have happened. Its foyers had wavy-patterned rubber floors with tubular steel settees. The auditorium, which seated over 2,000, was

decorated in warming peach tones with concealed lighting and turquoise curtains.

Similarly, W.R. Glen's **Regal** in Aberdeen lay abandoned – a granite-clad steel frame without a roof. When Glen died in 1951 after a long battle with cancer, his assistant Charles J. Foster took over a much-reduced ABC design office. He updated the cinema's design to incorporate elements of Festival of Britain influence. The pre-war streamlined look had been superseded by a new aesthetic – that of scientific symbolism. The structures of atoms and molecules, abstracted from physics and symbolising Britain's goal of advancement in the realms of science, technology and engineering, were combined with new finishes such as formica, mosaic and laminated plywood. For fashionable architects, the 1930s streamlined style was definitely passé. The Festival of Britain also deployed a new graphic identity, using a slanted font with heavy serifs. Many firms wanting to capture the spirit of the moment by associating themselves with the Festival's modernity adopted this. More fundamentally, the Festival promoted advanced building techniques through such space-age structures as the hovering Skylon and the vast clear span of the Dome of Discovery. While Foster's Aberdeen Regal was finished using the latest graphics, plenty of formica panelling, mosaic and terrazzo floors representing sodium crystals and walls studded with atomic patterns of lightbulbs, it was a lumpish building and nothing could disguise the fact that essentially it was a product of pre-war constructional thinking.

If George Palmer was one of a later generation of cinema circuit owners who only came to prominence in the post-war era, another was John B. Milne, who was born in 1902. He first entered the industry as a violinist in a cinema orchestra in Dundee before the advent of 'talkies.' He purchased his first cinema, the Palladium, in 1928 and expanded his circuit by taking over existing cinemas. In the late-1930s Milne controlled five cinemas in Dundee alone – the **Broadway**, **Regal**, **Palladium**, **Kinnaird** and **Victoria** – with other cinemas throughout Fife and Central Scotland. In 1941 he acquired the Gray's circuit when its original owner, C.R.W. Gray, died, giving him cinemas elsewhere in Angus as well and thus increasing his circuit size to 19. After the Second World War, the ambitious Milne wanted a city centre flagship, and so he acquired the site of the Majestic Picture Theatre in Seagate (see above), which had been gutted by fire. This he finally re-built and re-

The Kinnaird in Bank Street, Dundee was converted from an 1857-vintage public hall. Films were first shown in 1908 and it became a full-time cinema in 1920. By the 1950s, it was an important member of the J.B. Milne circuit. (George Millar)

On the site of the burned Majestic, Milne developed the Capitol (William M. Wilson, 1954) as a new flagship cinema but quickly sold it to ABC in exchange for cash and another property in the city. (Tony Moss collection, CTA Archive)

opened in 1956 as the **Capitol**. The project cost Milne £140,000, yet the outcome was an ugly building with a clumsy façade which was only distinguished by large slanted lettering in the then-fashionable 'Festival of Britain' style. It was, however, the first cinema in Dundee to be designed for the new wide-screen CinemaScope films, so it had a wide and shallow stadium-shaped auditorium with 1,300 seats to give the best viewing conditions for the new format, a vast screen and wall-to-wall gold curtains. Unfortunately, it seems that the architect, William M. Wilson, completely forgot to include a projection box in his plans and this was hastily added once construction was under way. Although successful at first, Milne found it ever harder to book the latest and best films as the large circuits tended to show these in their own cinemas, and so he arranged to swap the Capitol with ABC's elderly **Plaza** in Hilltown, giving ABC a city centre outlet in Dundee for the first time.

Television began to make serious inroads into cinema attendances during the 1960s. Hollywood, meanwhile, produced more adult-oriented films whose depiction of sex and violence, however tame by today's standards,

invariably attracted an X certificate, preventing children and young teenagers from gaining entry. The image of the cinema as a comfortable and friendly resort, to which the whole family could escape, began to fade. Fights and vandalism made some of the declining picture-houses nightmarish to manage and inevitably deterred respectable patrons (the Lyceum in Edinburgh, Green's Playhouse in Wishaw and ABC's Rex in Riddrie seem to have been particularly badly affected – was it a coincidence that Barlinnie Jail was only a short distance away from the latter?).

To combat the increasing popularity of television (which had made an earlier impact in the United States), a number of new cinema processes were developed by the different Hollywood studios and were greeted by the British cinema trade with enthusiasm, even though their proliferation in the early 1950s was at a time when exhibitors could least afford them. Three-dimensional films (3D) were introduced at selected city centre cinemas in 1953, but for satisfactory presentation this demanded the exact synchronisation of two projectors and two spares for the change-over of reels (almost all

Above: An X-rated film called 'The Sinner' comes to the Elephant cinema in Shawlands on Glasgow's South Side (H. Barnes, 1927). X-certified films were disastrous for such large venues as they excluded family audiences and so broke their weekly cinema-going habit. The Elephant was originally a member of the eccentric A.E. Pickard's circuit – hence the unusual name. (Bruce Peter collection)
Below: The auditorium of the Coliseum Cinerama in Glasgow after rebuilding in 1962. (Bruce Peter collection)
Bottom right: A new CinemaScope installation in the former Radio (now George) in Kilbirnie in the mid-1950s. George Palmer invested heavily in his cinemas and, here, an entirely new proscenium has been installed. (Bruce Peter collection)

cinemas had only two of these expensive items). A specially-coated screen had to be fitted and the audience supplied with special glasses, which had to be cleaned after every show. Cinerama was even more complicated and necessitated the complete demolition of existing cinema interiors where it was installed as a giant 180-degree curved screen had to be fitted around the front of the auditorium and three projection booths had to be perfectly synchronised. In 1962 ABC's **Coliseum** in Glasgow underwent an ill-conceived, million pound alteration into Scotland's only Cinerama theatre. The auditorium was completely transformed into a 1,310 seat hall with only one balcony below a suspended ceiling and wall-to-wall curtaining over the gigantic screen. During this conversion, a corrugated metal frontispiece was slapped onto the old sandstone façade.

Cinerama films were strong on spectacle but poor on narrative content, and so few British cinemas converted. The first performance of *How The West Was Won*, nonetheless, was warmly received at the Coliseum Cinerama on 26 September 1963 and, perhaps not surprisingly in a tough district like the Gorbals, *The Dirty*

Dozen also did well, but Cinerama was not a lasting success in Glasgow. By the seventies Cinerama films were no longer being made and the Coliseum reverted to normal programmes. Besides, such gimmicks did not hold the public's imagination for long.

Stereophonic sound, on the other hand, had everything to recommend it, except cost, and it too was installed in the more prestigious city centre cinemas and a few better-class suburban venues. Of all the innovations, wide-screen films in CinemaScope or Todd-AO proved to be of the most immediate value. The former required anamorphic lenses to widen the image but was an immediate success when premièred at the **New Victoria** in Edinburgh and **Gaumont** (formerly The Picture House) in Glasgow. As the large suburban cinemas of the 1930s had been designed with wide-screen processes in mind, the conversion was simple enough. In older cinemas with proscenium openings to fit the old 1.33:1 aspect ratio, the owners could either completely re-build the interior with a new, wide proscenium end – as happened at the **New Cinema**, Airdrie – or, alternatively, simply lower the top masking to achieve a wide image smaller than what had gone before, thus defeating the point of the exercise – as happened at the **Pavilion** in the same town. With limited cash available,

cinema owners faced a dilemma. On the one hand, they could not afford a costly investment in what might turn out to be a short-lived craze but, on the other hand, they could not afford to be late in adopting a means of increasing and maintaining dwindling audiences.

Other cinemas declined with slum clearance and comprehensive redevelopment. Those that directly escaped the bulldozers through compulsory purchase orders were also doomed as local populations were thinned and their audiences were moved to new peripheral suburbs. Glasgow was particularly affected in this regard. As complete districts were razed to the ground, shops, cinemas and other services attempted to cater for the few that remained in the hope that, once redevelopment work was complete, the cinema-going habit would also return. However, people living in high-rise flats and maisonettes tended not to go out for their entertainment as before. There was more space to relax in new post-war homes and the ever-present lure of television, and so cinema owners faced meagre returns.

In 1955 it was estimated in the *Ideal Kinema* that a full CinemaScope installation with stereophonic sound would cost £640 for projector lenses, screen material at £1 per square foot, proscenium remodelling at between £850 and £2,500 and a stereophonic sound system at between

Demolition of the Roxy in Glasgow's Maryhill Road in 1962. The tram lines have gone and, in the background, new high-rise flats are taking shape. (CTA Archive)

The Regal in Stirling is torn down in March 1968 to make way for a road-widening scheme. (A. Ernest Glen)

£2,500 and £4,000. With average box office returns estimated at £15,653 (net of Entertainment Tax) in a typical cinema, no wonder the industry was gloomy. As J. Arthur Rank had predicted, mass cinema closures began in 1955, mainly of poorer quality venues. This was a direct result of the introduction of commercial television. (Incidentally, the ABC and Granada cinema chains both successfully acquired ITV franchises for Birmingham and Manchester respectively, while in Scotland the cinema owner Sir A.B. King became the founding Chairman of Scottish Television.)

When gaming laws were relaxed in 1961 to allow bingo, this new craze quickly swept the country. Many cinemas, particularly independently-run suburban venues, at first switched to bingo, not because films were losing money but because bingo promised much greater profits, augmented by bars, buffet counters and gaming on fruit machines. Cinemas became bingo halls with the minimum of effort – new direct lighting in the auditorium to enable customers to strike off their books, a gaudy new paint scheme and the conversion of the stalls to a seats-around-tables configuration. Thanks to bingo, many cinemas of architectural significance have remained otherwise intact.

The two major national circuits – Rank and ABC – did little to help the situation during the 1950s and 1960s. While they could have done nothing to prevent some decline due to television and other factors, they could at least have slowed it by having a better choice of films. Many British releases were judged by their takings in London's West End during exclusive runs prior to nation-wide release. There, perhaps due to the more liberal morality of a large metropolis, or simply the presence of

Soho, films with a distinctly 'adult' theme tended to do well. Apart from the giants around Leicester Square, many West End cinemas were small and better suited to speciality films which inevitably attracted an X certificate, excluding family audiences. When these transferred to suburban 'super' cinemas around the country with over 2,000 seats to fill, they were disastrous. These cinemas relied for their success on popular appeal to family audiences which this trend substantially impaired. Each circuit cinema in any given area tended to show the same programme and, as more of the audience had cars, this was hardly a far-sighted policy. If the ABC release happened to have an X certificate one week, every ABC cinema in any given area would be showing the same film. The cinemas were already often scruffy and now they gained a reputation for being sleazy as well. Their cafés, which earned additional money and had been genteel retreats for ladies to meet for a chat during shopping trips, became no-go areas and closed by the score.

Yet, some well-located city centre cinemas remained

A bingo session in progress in the Vogue in Govan in the 1970s. Bingo became the great preserver of cinema buildings which would otherwise have been demolished.

Green's Playhouse in Wishaw is a well-maintained and impressive Mecca bingo hall. Thanks to 'the numbers game', it is possible still to enjoy the scale and ambition of the auditorium, once one of Scotland's largest cinemas. Today, bingo has often moved out of old cinemas into purpose-built 'leisure sheds' as these are easier to maintain and enable superior disabled access. (Bruce Peter)

popular. ABC's Glasgow Regal had always been busy – so much so that in October 1967 ABC opened Glasgow's first entirely new post-war cinema, the unimaginatively named **ABC 2** next door, renaming the Regal the **ABC 1** at the same time. The 922 seat ABC 2 was a charmless edifice of brown brick, relieved only by two rows of small square windows, an upper roof level clad in copper and, above the street, a canopy stretching the full length of the façade. Inside there was a bar, a coffee lounge in the foyer and an admittedly impressive semicircular auditorium with an enormous screen covered by wall-to-wall gold curtains.

In the sixties, concerts supplemented films at many of Rank's larger theatres (the Gaumonts and Odeons) as these often guaranteed a bigger audience and greater profitability than a weak film. Thus, the Beatles and the Rolling Stones made early appearances at the Glasgow Odeon. Bill Beattie, then an assistant projectionist, has fond memories of these concerts:

'The Beatles came to the Odeon even before they were really famous. I think their last tour date had been in Elgin Town Hall! Anyway, they were real troupers and played to a packed and hysterical audience at the Odeon. Roy Orbison once shared the bill with the 'Fab Four' and we could have sold that show for months.'

In 1970 Rank chose to close their other central Glasgow cinemas and concentrate film shows at the Odeon. A comprehensive reconstruction, involving the complete demolition of the existing interior, created three new, smaller auditoria. Unlike their Art Deco predecessor, the new Odeons were rather bland, but the interior changes were as nothing compared to the indignities heaped on the exterior. The five tall windows and eye-catching fins of the former Paramount (see above) were unforgivably covered in cheap, grey corrugated sheet metal and a vertical readograph of insensitive proportions was placed centrally above a monstrous new canopy. If the architects, Dry Halasz Dixon – why not name the guilty? – had intended completely to hide the original grand design, they failed. The additions appeared to be just what they were: ugly indiscretions tacked onto the original stonework. While these efforts destroyed the cinema's aesthetic interest, they did wonders for Rank's profits. In a joint ceremony, the three screens were opened on 2 October 1970 by the triplets Elizabeth, Glenda and Margaret Crammond and, true to previous form, the **Odeon Film Centre** became Britain's busiest cinema. In 1986, Screens 2 and 3 were further subdivided to make a six-screen complex. The Regal in Edinburgh was similarly re-built by C.J. Foster as the **ABC Film Centre** with three screens. This conversion was better designed than that of the Glasgow Odeon, but nonetheless it obliterated

Above: The ABC 2 in Glasgow's Sauchiehall Street (C.J. Foster, 1967) was externally a dreary brown brick edifice in late modernist style. The former Regal, adjacent, has become the ABC 1. (Bruce Peter collection)

Above: The 'space age' foyer of the ABC Film Centre in Edinburgh (C.J. Foster, 1969), formerly the Regal (for comparison, see page 109). (Bruce Peter collection)

Left: The ABC 1 auditorium in the Edinburgh ABC Film Centre with wall-to-wall curtaining covering a large CinemaScope screen. (Bruce Peter collection)

Top left: The foyer of the Odeon Film Centre in Glasgow (Dry Halasz Dixon, 1970). (Bruce Peter collection)

Top right: The bar in the Odeon Film Centre can be compared with the same space in the Paramount, shown on page 94. (Bruce Peter collection)

Centre: Odeon 1 in the Odeon Film Centre, finished in rough-textured plaster for acoustic reasons but completely lacking in ornamentation. It did however provide excellent viewing conditions with a large screen and good sight-lines. (Bruce Peter collection)

Bottom left: The Odeon Film Centre in the latter 1970s; the grey corrugated metal additions are most unattractive (see page 94 for the original design). (Chris Doak)

Bottom right: The opening night of the Odeon Film Centre on 2 October 1970. (Bruce Peter collection)

all evidence of W.R. Glen's wonderful 1938 interior.

Caledonian Associated Cinemas built new cinemas hardly worthy of mention as adjuncts to shopping malls to serve the new towns of East Kilbride and Livingston and refurbished others. The firm unwisely tried to emulate ABC by renaming its **Cinema** in Dunfermline the **CAC**! Otherwise, none was built in Scotland until 1988 when the first entirely new multiplex – the **AMC** (American Multi Cinemas) – opened in Clydebank with ten screens. The multiplex was at first slow to catch on in Britain, where planners were initially suspicious of allowing further suburban sprawl of Californian proportions. However, redundant former industrial land, so-called brown field sites, freed up by the early 1980s recession, proved to be ideal for this kind of development. More quickly followed and these projects helped to make one Glasgow architects' firm a potent – and now global – force in recent cinema design. Unick Architects (formerly Howard & Unick) got involved first by subdividing existing cinemas, such as the ABC 1 in Glasgow's Sauchiehall Street, which they carved into four screens, before riding the multiplex boom. In Glasgow they designed the **Cannon Cinemas** at The Forge Shopping Centre, Parkhead, opened in 1989. Today, the firm is one of the world's most productive designers of these buildings with projects churned out everywhere from Germany to Argentina, but it keeps a low profile: an omnipotent but, to the public, an almost invisible force in the re-shaping of urban space.

The **Showcase Cinemas** multiplexes in Coatbridge and Paisley typify the multiplex genre in its 'leisure park' incarnation. Set amid acres of depressing, windswept car park with American-style fast food outlets dotted around its distant perimeter, a typical Showcase Cinema is clad in grey cement blockwork. Above its entrance is a display of 'neon art.' Unlike earlier generations of cinema, where the neon emphasised the building's composition at night, this appears as an afterthought bearing no relationship to the architecture. Instead, the observer can only conclude that it is there in a vain attempt to cheer up an otherwise hopelessly dismal warehouse-like edifice. Inside, the foyer is expansive and appears efficiently laid out with strategically-located food and drink stalls selling mainly popcorn, burgers and cola. The space is white-painted and has grey carpet tiles. The auditoria, in contrast, are black and without screen tabs, but the sight-lines, the sound quality and the seat comfort are near perfect.

In the mid-1990s, planning guidelines changed to make such land-hungry out-of-town developments more difficult to encourage developments back into city centres. Theoretically, this should also have brought about a better standard of design. With few exceptions, sadly, this has not been the case. There was some excitement when Virgin Cinemas announced that the former Green's Playhouse site between Glasgow's Renfield and West Nile Streets was again to host Britain's biggest cinema – a 'megaplex.' While under construction, the Virgin chain was sold to **UGC**, under which name it opened in 2001. Even before opening, its cynical, architecturally illiterate expanses of brown and cream rainscreen cladding had won it *Prospect Magazine*'s controversial 'Carbuncle' award for Scotland's ugliest new building. It is only reasonable to wonder how this could have happened.

One argument goes like this: when people are genuinely impoverished or have limited resources, they are inspired by the prospect of going to seek entertainment in luxurious settings – hence the

The 14-screen Showcase Cinemas multiplex near Coatbridge. Inside the windows, there is 'neon art' – but this appears to have been added as an afterthought in an attempt to cheer up what is a rather dreary edifice. (Bruce Peter)

popularity of 'picture palaces' and 'super' cinemas during the Depression-struck 1930s and the austerity of the Second World War. Today's teenagers, in contrast, are products of a far wealthier consumer society, coming from comfortable homes and often with house-proud parents. Consequently they look for escapism in night clubs with 'underground' names and ambience such as 'The Tunnel' and 'The Garage.' Perhaps the trashy design of the multiplex cinema fulfils a similar social function. This, however, certainly does not excuse the unforgivably low level of architectural aspiration demonstrated by the majority of specialist multiplex cinema designers today. Rather, it demonstrates that the functionality of cinema buildings is as complex as the public's taste is fickle.

More likely, the global entertainment conglomerates which control most cinemas today have either forgotten, or choose to ignore, the need to build creatively. In the 1930s, cinema circuits tended to be the brainchilds of entrepreneurs who took a patriarchal pride in providing buildings of distinction. Describing the architecture of his Odeon cinemas in *Architectural Design and Construction* in March 1937, Oscar Deutsch was very specific:

'…It was always my ambition to have buildings which were individual and striking, but which were always objects of architectural beauty… We endeavour to make our buildings express the fact that they are specially erected as the homes of the latest, most progressive entertainment in the world today… I am determined, and every member of my organisation from the highest to the lowest is fully aware of the fact, that every future theatre we build will be better…than its predecessor. I am…determined that the buildings…will be worthy of the purpose to which they are put.'

For Deutsch, the cinema architecture was vital to his promotion of Odeon's corporate brand identity, whereas developers nowadays appear to be obsessed by brand alone. In the 1930s, Deutsch's Odeons became British architectural icons but, although the chain continues under new owners, its recent multiplexes show little of the old ambition. Odeon, we are told, is 'Fanatical About Film', but one would hardly know this to look at its latest developments, such as the **Odeon** multiplex in Kilmarnock – a grey metal shed isolated amid windswept car parks.

As we have seen, however, there is a long tradition of disparagement towards recent cinema architecture. In the 1930s, the prominence and decorative eclecticism of cinemas made them equally vulnerable to criticism. At the 1935 Royal Institute of British Architects Conference, Professor Harold Hughes lambasted cafés, public houses, cinemas, ice rinks and hotels as 'spurious modern work, put out merely for effect', condemning 'the craving for novelty and advertisement.' He continued: 'The majority of modern buildings are produced merely to be novel, to catch the eye and to become easily notorious.'

Cinema is fast-moving in every sense and, moreover, it is a popular medium – rarely achieving the status of high art. Back in the 1930s, the architect and academic H.S. Goodhart-Rendel, a man never short of a well-turned phrase, observed that 'too much stylishness makes an unkind frame for a scene or picture that will most often have no stylishness whatsoever.' Popular art and popular culture are dictated by the taste of the moment and cinemas exemplify this in architecture – fashionable, ephemeral buildings which burst onto the townscape promising the latest in modernity, before falling slowly out of favour.

The Odeon in Kilmarnock, which opened in 1998, is entirely faced in grey rainscreen cladding – not very appealing on a typically grey and wet Scottish day. (Bruce Peter)

The Architects and Interior Decorators

+ Indicates that the cinema has been entirely demolished

Alexander, John (Newcastle)

Of M. Alexander & Son, Newcastle (fibrous plaster manufacturers). Alexander himself was an accomplished interior decorator who specialised in the design, manufacture and supply of fibrous plasterwork, particularly for cinema interiors. Alexander's work constituted some of the richest and most flamboyant Art Deco interior designs produced in 1930s Britain. These he represented with beautifully rendered water-colour paintings (many of which survive in the Victoria & Albert Museum). The majority of Alexander's cinema schemes were to be found around his native Newcastle-upon-Tyne, but he also devised a number of schemes for Scottish cinemas. Alas, nearly all of his interiors have been destroyed or severely mutilated and only one, the Northwick in Worcester, remains in original condition. Scottish projects included Green's Playhouse, Dundee (1936) + and the Regal, Bathgate (1938).

Arthur, George (Airdrie)

An Airdrie-based architect who designed a wide variety of building types in a chunky Beaux Arts manner (perhaps best described as 'Lanarkshire Municipal'). Theatre and cinema projects include the Olympia Theatre (Bridgeton) Glasgow (1911) with the office of Frank Matcham and an un-built cinema (1912) at 727 Govan Road, Glasgow.

Atkinson, Robert (London)

1883-1952. Atkinson was a forward-looking and distinguished man well-connected in the London architecture scene who studied architecture in Nottingham, travelling also to Paris, Italy and America, where he became interested in cinema design. Principal of the Architecture Association School from 1913. Director of the AA School 1920-29. Designer of several very important cinemas, including The Picture House, Edinburgh +; The Picture House, Aberdeen + and, above all, the Regent, Brighton +. A key figure in the London architecture 'establishment' during the 1930s and a keen advocate of progressive design.

Baird Jnr, Thomas (Glasgow)

Green's Picturedrome, Ballater Street, Glasgow (1911) +; Camphill Picture House, Baker Street, Glasgow (1912) +; Avenue, Dumbarton Road, Glasgow (1912) +; Salon, Sauchiehall Street, Glasgow (1913) +.

Barclay, David (Glasgow)

1846-1917. Son of Hugh Barclay (of Barclay & Watt). Designer of several other schools and churches in and around Glasgow; Lyceum Theatre, Govan (1899) +.

Blain, William J. of Denny & Blain (Dumbarton)

The Tivoli Cinema, Partick, Glasgow (1929) +; un-built, Cumbernauld Road, Glasgow (1929).

Boswell, George A. (Glasgow)

1879-1952. Former chief assistant to James Miller, under whose direction he was designer of the Argyle Electric Cinema (1910). Designer of at least 14 cinemas. Lived in the White House of Milliken which he converted, and wore orange clothes (according to Charles McKean's *The Scottish Thirties*). Panopticon (alterations), Trongate, Glasgow (1906); Govan Rink, Summerstown Road, Govan (1909) +; Charing Cross Electric Theatre, Sauchiehall Street, Glasgow (1910); Argyle Electric, Argyle Street, Glasgow (1910) +; Bridgeton Cross Electric Theatre, Olympia Street, Glasgow (1910) +; Casino, Castle Street, Glasgow (1911) +; St. Enoch Picture Theatre, Argyle Street, Glasgow (1912); Paisley Picture Theatre (1913) +; Seamore, Maryhill Road, Glasgow (1914) +; un-built cinema, Main Street, Pollokshaws, Glasgow (1914); Black Cat, Springfield Road, Glasgow (1921); Grand, Cowcaddens Street, Glasgow (1926) +; Eastwood Secondary School, Williamfield (1936); two extensions to Templeton's Carpet Factory, Glasgow (1934-38); Argyle, Argyle Street, Glasgow (1938); Premises of Newall Ltd, Possil, Glasgow (1940). From 1952 firm continued as Boswell, Mitchell & Johnston.

Brand & Lithgow (Glasgow)

Technically innovative practice which made some of the first uses of reinforced concrete in the city. Sentinel Works, King's Park (with Archibald Leitch) – the earliest reinforced concrete-framed structure in Glasgow (1903);. Partick Masonic Hall, Ardery Street,

Glasgow (1910); Hillhead Salon, Vinicambe Street, Glasgow (1912); Granville, Great Western Road, Glasgow (1920) +.

Cattanach, Col. Alexander (Kingussie)

c1857-1938. Meadowside Hospital, Kincraig (1906); Duke of Gordon Hotel, Kingussie (1906); Kingussie U.F. Church (1908-09); Playhouse cinema, Perth (1933); Playhouse cinema, Keith (1935) +; Playhouse cinema, Fraserburgh (1937) +.

Crewe, Bertie (London)

Prolific and outstanding theatre architect, trained in the *Ecole des Beaux Arts*. Initially in partnership with W.G.R. Sprague. Designer of theatres and cinemas throughout England, including several of the most important in London's West End. Scottish works include the Paisley Theatre (1890) (with Sprague) +; the Pavilion Theatre, Glasgow (1904); the Palace Theatre, Glasgow (1904) + and Bostock's Zoo Hippodrome and Grand Variety Circus, Cowcaddens, Glasgow (1897). All of Crewe's Scottish buildings showed films at one time or another.

Cullen, Alexander of Cullen, Lochead & Brown (Hamilton)

1857-1911. Prolific Lanarkshire architect who designed many of Hamilton's important public buildings, mainly in an imposing 'municipal baroque' idiom. Works include Hamilton Police Station (1894); Brandon Chambers, Hamilton (1898); Parish Council offices, Hamilton (1900); Carnegie Library, Coatbridge (1905); Hamilton Municipal Buildings (1906-14). Towards the end of his career, Cullen's firm developed a penchant for Art Nouveau and this is most evident in the three theatres he designed for the R.C. Buchanan circuit: the New Century Theatre, Motherwell (1902) +; the Grand Theatre, Falkirk (1903) + and the King's Theatre, Kilmarnock (1904).

Duff, Neil C. of Duff & Cairns (Glasgow)

1861-1934. Ibrox Cinematograph Theatre, Lendel Place, Glasgow (1910) +; Electric Picture Palace, Maryhill Road, Glasgow (1910) +; Royal, Springburn Road, Glasgow (1910) +; Cinema Picture House, Renfield Street, Glasgow (1911) +; Empire, Titchfield Street, Kilmarnock (1912) +; Electric, Cornwall Street, Glasgow (1912) +; La Scala, Sauchiehall Street, Glasgow (1912); La Scala, Helensburgh (1913); Lorne, Cornwall Street, Glasgow (1914) +; Rosevale, Dumbarton Road, Glasgow (1920); un-built, Bank

Street, Glasgow (1920); Panoptican (alterations), Trongate, Glasgow (1920); Cinema Picture House (alterations), Renfield Street, Glasgow (1920) +; Marne, Marne Street, Glasgow (1921) +; Grafton, Parliamentary Road, Glasgow (1922) +; Carlton, Castle Street, Glasgow (1926) +; Picture House (alterations) Falkirk (1927); Waldorf Dance Hall, Sauchiehall Street, Glasgow (1928).

Emberton, Joseph (London)

1889-1956. Emberton was born in Audley in Staffordshire. His ability to adapt modernism to the needs of entertainment and his eye for detail led to his being retained as the official architect to Blackpool Pleasure Beach, updating it on a piecemeal basis, until his death. In the cinema line, he designed only the façade, foyer and café of Green's Playhouse, Dundee (with John Fairweather) (1936) +.

Fairweather, John & Son (Glasgow)

1867-1942. Fairweather visited USA in 1922 to study cinema theatre design. His son, W. John Fairweather, born 1908, joined the practice in the mid-1920s. 14 cinemas including the Edinburgh Playhouse and the Green's Playhouses, Dundee and Glasgow – the three largest cinemas in Scotland, two of them the largest in Europe. The output of the practice was devoted to planning of cinemas and private houses only. They included Roller Coaster, Vinegarhill (1910); Vitagraph, Sauchiehall Street, Glasgow (1912); Green's Picturedome, Summerstown Road, Glasgow (1912) +; La Scala, Saltcoats (1912); Green's Picturedrome, Wellshot Road, Glasgow (1914) +; Green's Pavilion, Rutherglen (1914) +; Kings (ex Vitagraph) (alterations), Sauchiehall Street, Glasgow (1914); Capital, Lorne Street, Glasgow (1927); Green's Playhouse, Renfield Street, Glasgow (1927) +; Savoy, Cambuslang (1928); Regal, Dalmuir (alterations) (1929) +; Playhouse, Edinburgh (1929); King's, Perth (1930); Green's Playhouse, Ayr (1931); Palladium (alterations), Paisley (1932) +; Rex, Lockerbie (1932); La Scala, Aberdeen (1933) +; East Park Home School, Glasgow (1933); Ritz, Burton-on-Trent (1935); The British Linen Company, Gallowgate, Glasgow (1936); Regal, Saltcoats (1936); Grange, Stevenston (1936) +; Playhouse, Colchester (1936); Auditorium of Green's Playhouse, Dundee (1936) +; Rex, Campbeltown (1937) +; Playhouse, Wigan (1938).

Foster, C.J. (London)

C.J. (Jack) Foster replaced William R. Glen as ABC's chief architect, following the latter's death in 1951.

Foster's cinema designs for ABC are characterised by a dreary commercial form of late modernism – albeit with impressive auditoria, designed to show off the then new wide-screen processes to best effect. Regal, Aberdeen +; conversion of ABC Coliseum, Glasgow, to Coliseum Cinerama +; conversion of Regal, Glasgow to ABC 1 and design of adjacent ABC 2.

Gardner, Albert V. (and Glen & Thomson) (Glasgow)

Gardner was a highly eclectic and eccentric architect who produced, in the main, very inexpensively-constructed cinemas of dubious quality for operators catering mainly to the 'lower end' of the cinema market. By the late-1920s, Gardner had begun to design 'atmospheric' cinemas and these represented his best work. Some projects he designed alone, but for a period in the late-1920s and early-1930s he worked on a few projects in conjunction with W.R. Glen. These were all for companies in which John Maxwell of ABC was involved and Glen later became ABC's house architect, based in London. Altogether, Gardner was involved in 36 cinemas including: Cinema De Luxe, Sauchiehall Street, Glasgow (1911) +; Majestic, Inglefield Street, Glasgow (1912) +; Avenue, Dumbarton Road, Glasgow (1913) +; Partick Picture House, Orchard Street, Glasgow (1913) +; Scenic, Paisley Road, Glasgow (1913) +; New Star, Maryhill Road, Glasgow (1913) +; Vaudeville, Argyle Street, Glasgow (1914) +; Picture House, Dunoon (1914) +; Grove, Breadalbane Street, Glasgow (1915) +; Queens, Battlefield Road, Glasgow (1916) +; Elder, Rathlin Street, Glasgow (1916) +; Possilpark Picture House, Saracen Street, Glasgow (1920) +; Springburn Picture House, Wellfield Street, Glasgow (1920) +; New Alex Picture House, Paisley (1921) +; un-built, Bankhall Street, Glasgow (1921); Picture House, Greenock (1921) +; Grosvenor, Byres Road, Glasgow (1921) (with W.R. Glen); Standard (alterations), Dumbarton Road, Glasgow (1922) +; Coliseum (alterations), Eglinton Street, Glasgow (1925) +; Paragon (alterations), Cumberland Street, Glasgow (1925) +; West End Cinema, Paisley (1925) +; Kinema, Springburn Road, Glasgow (1926) +; Wellington Palace (alterations), Commercial Road, Glasgow (1927) +; Lorne (alterations), Cornwall Street, Glasgow (1928) +; Strathclyde, Summerfield Street, Glasgow (1928) +; Ritz, Rodney Street, Edinburgh (1929) +; un-built, Lauderdale Gardens, Glasgow (1929); Kelvin, Argyle Street, Glasgow (1930) (with W.R. Glen) +; New Star (alterations), Maryhill Road, Glasgow (1930) +; Partick Picture House (alterations), Orchard Street, Glasgow (1931) +; Astoria, Possil Road, Glasgow (1931) +; Orient, Ayr (1932); Orient, Gallowgate, Glasgow

(1933) +; Picture House (alterations), Campbeltown (1934); Grand Central (alterations), Jamaica Street, Glasgow (1938).

Gibson, Thomas Bowhill (Edinburgh)

1895-1949. Rutland, Edinburgh (1930) +; Rio Cinema, Kirkcaldy (1937) +; Rio Cinema, Craigmillar, Edinburgh (1938) +; Dominion Cinema, Morningside, Edinburgh (1939); County Cinema, Portobello (1939); Learmonth flats, Edinburgh (1935); Roadhouse, Granton, Edinburgh ; Hillburn Inn and private houses.

Gillespie, James and Scott, James (St Andrews)

1854-1914 and 1861-1944. St Andrews Post Office (1892); Kirkcaldy Sheriff Court (1894); St Andrews University Hall (1895-96); other churches, schools and public buildings in and around St Andrews; New Picture House, St Andrews (1930).

Glen, William Riddell (Glasgow and London)

1884-1951. Principally cinema architect. From 1930, house architect to ABC cinemas. Glen's office was based at ABC's Golden Square headquarters in London. Most of Glen's cinema output was henceforth in England. As assistant to J.A. Campbell: Queen Victoria Memorial School, Dunblane. With Albert V. Gardner: Grosvenor Cinema, Hillhead, Glasgow (1921); Strathclyde Cinema, Dalmarnock, Glasgow (1929) +; Ritz Cinema, Edinburgh (1929) +. In charge of ABC's architects department: Forum, Birmingham (converted Masonic Hall) (1930); Savoy, Brighton (1930); Coliseum, Glasgow (alterations to enlarge capacity of existing ex-theatre) (1931) +; Forum, Liverpool (with A. Ernest Shennan) (1931); Elephant & Castle Theatre (re-build of variety theatre) (1932); Savoy, Wandsworth (1932) +; Regal, Torquay (1933) +; Ritz, Vicar Lane, Leeds (1934) +; Forum, Southampton (1935); Regal, Wakefield (1935) +: Regal, Walham Green (1935) +; Savoy, Stoke Newington, London (1936); Savoy, Croydon (1936); Savoy, Exeter (1936) +; Regal, Chesterfield (J. Owen Bond with alterations by Glen) (1936); Regal, Hackney, London (1936) +; Regal, Hammersmith, London (1936) +; Savoy, Lincoln (1936) +; Rex, Leytonstone, London (1936) +; Ritz, Muswell Hill, London (1936) +; Savoy, Northampton (1936); Westover, Bournemouth (1937); Regal, Chester (1937); Regal, Grimsby (1937); Regal, Harrogate (with H. Linley-Brown) (1937) +; Regal, Hounslow, London (1937) +; Regal, Ilford (1937); Savoy, Leicester (1937); Regal, Levenshulme, Manchester (1937); Regal, Old Kent Road, London (1937) +; Savoy, Portsmouth (1937) +; Regal, Putney, London (1937) +; Regal,

Salisbury (1937); Ritz, Sunderland (1937); Savoy, Swindon (1937); Savoy, Teddington (1937) +; Regal, Wembley, London (1937) +; Savoy, Wolverhampton (1937) +; Regal, York (with Penty & Thompson) (1937) +; Savoy, Birkenhead (1938) +; Regent, Chatham (1938) +; Regal, Derby (1938) +; Regal, Edgware Rd, London (1938) +; Regal, Edinburgh (with Stewart Kaye of Stewart Kaye & Walls) (1938) +; Regal, Halifax (1938); Regent, Knotty Ash, Liverpool (1938) +; Regal, Leigh, Manchester (1938) +; Ritz, Leyton, London (1938); Savoy, Luton (1938); Royal, Plymouth (1938); Regal, Rochdale (with Leslie C. Norton) (1938); Ritz, Romford (1938) +; Savoy, Walsall (1938) +; Regal, Streatham, London (1938); Regal, Southport (1938) +; Gaiety, Aston, Birmingham (with C.J. Foster) (1939) +; Ritz, Bradford (1939) +; Regal, Cheltenham (with Leslie C. Norton) (1939) +; Ritz, Clapton, London (1939) +; Adelphi, Dublin (with W.R. Donnelly) (1939); Empire, Mile End, London (1939); Carlton, Nottingham (1939) +; Regal, Twickenham, London (1939) +; Regal, Staines (1939) +; Palace, Arbroath (1940) +; Rex, Bedminster, Bristol (1940); Regal, Camberwell, London (with Leslie Kemp) (1940); Savoy, Holloway, London (1940); Regal, Aberdeen (pre-war Glen shell with post-war Foster interior) (1939-1954) +; Regal, Gloucester (pre-war shell by Glen completed by W.R. Farrow) (1939-1954).

Haxton, Andrew David (Leven)

Born 1878. A partner in Haxton & Walker of Leven (William Walker 1881-1923). Leven Public School (1910-11); Methil Community Centre (1926-27); Semi-detached houses, Elie (1930-33); St Peta's RC Church Hall, Leven (1925); Miners' Welfare Hall, Lochgelly (1923-25); Nurses' Home, Stratheden Hospital, Cupar (1929); Troxy, Leven (1936); Regal, Broxburn (1937) +; Regal, Armadale (1937) +; Regal, Bathgate (1938).

Houston, James (Kilbirnie)

1893-1966. Work includes the Moorings, Largs (1935) +; Radio Cinema, Kilbirnie (1936); the Viking Cinema, Largs (1939) + and several Galbraith stores (eg Milngavie 1939). Many houses and light industrial units. Lecturer at the Glasgow School of Art.

Inglis, William Beresford (Glasgow)

Cinema architect. promoter and owner. Designer also of some pubs, houses in Whitecraigs; managing director, designer and owner of the Beresford Hotel. The firm was originally Weddell & Inglis and continued as Weddell & Thompson. Arcadia, London Road, Glasgow (1920) +; Ritz, Oatlands, Glasgow (converted from Oatlands Hippodrome) (1921) +; Imperial, Govan Road, Glasgow (1921); Boulevard, Knightscliffe Avenue, Glasgow (1928) +; Ritz, Cambuslang (1930) +; Toledo, Clarkston Road, Glasgow (1933); Ferrari's Restaurant, Glasgow (1933) +; St Charles Roman Catholic School, Glasgow (1934); Rogano Oyster Bar, Glasgow (1936); the Boundary Bar, Springburn, Glasgow (1937); Beresford Hotel, Glasgow (1938).

Laird, J W and Napier (Glasgow)

J. Austen Laird, son of J.W. Laird. Star Cinema, Main Street, Bridgeton, Glasgow (1908) +; Empress, Ballater Street, Gorbals, Glasgow (1912) +; Winner of *Daily Mail* 1931 competition for a Scottish house; Robertson Dunn headquarters at Temple; Norwood Cinema (1936); Ladykin School, Greenock (1930); Bay Hotel, Gourock (1938) +.

Lennox, Gavin and McMath, Daniel W. (Glasgow)

Designers of 8 cinemas in and around Glasgow including the Regal, Dumbarton (1923) +; New Bedford, Eglinton Street, Glasgow (1924) +; Oxford, Keppochill Road, Glasgow (1927) +; Florida, Ardmay Crescent, Glasgow (1929) +; Crown, Crown Street, Glasgow (1930) +; Roxy, Maryhill Road, Glasgow (1930) +; New Bedford, Eglinton Street, Glasgow (1932); Granada, Duke Street, Glasgow (1935) +; Tudor, Giffnock (1936) +; Rex, Newmilns (1936) +; Eclipse (completed post-war as the Plaza), Port Glasgow (1937); Globe Cinema, Johnstone (1939). Also Eaglesham School (1940); Masonic Temple, Queen Street, Renfrew (1931).

Mather, Andrew (London)

1891-1938. A London-based architect whose practice was responsible for many Odeon cinemas in the South of England. When, in the latter-1930s, Odeon decided to expand in Scotland, it was Mather's office which designed the cinemas. Those at Motherwell, Hamilton and Ayr were the work of Thomas Braddock, while un-built schemes elsewhere were designed by Keith Roberts. Odeon, Motherwell (1938) +; Odeon, Hamilton (1938) +; Odeon, Ayr (1938); plus un-built schemes for Odeon, Bridgeton; Odeon, Partick; Odeon, Townhead; Odeon, Dumbarton and Odeon, Falkirk.

MacDonald, Alister (London)

1898-1993. Son of Prime Minister Ramsay MacDonald. Designer of several cinemas including: Plaza, Lower Regent Street, London (Clerk of Works to architects

Verity & Beverley during construction) (1925-26); Leicester Square Theatre, London (alterations) (1931); Sphere News Theatre (Tottenham Court Road, London (1931) +; Playhouse, Elgin (1932); Playhouse, Montrose (1933) +; Victoria Station News Theatre, London (1933) +; Playhouse, Peebles (1933); Waterloo Station News Theatre, London (1934) +; Broadway, Prestwick (1935); Mayfair, Old Bury Road, Besses o' th' Barns, Lancs (1936); Cinenews, Commercial Road, Portsmouth (1936) +; Cinenews, High Street, Tooting, London (1936) +; Lyceum, Dumfries (1936) +; Cameo, Victoria Street, London (1937) +; Cinenews, Above Bar, Southampton (1937) +; Playhouse, Buckie (1937); Empire, Glasgow Empire Exhibition, Bellahouston Park (1938) +; Peace Cairn, Empire Exhibition, Bellahouston Park (1938); Cinema, Seria, Borneo (1953); Vanbrugh Theatre, Gower Street, London (1954); Comedy Theatre, Panton Street, London (alterations) (1955).

MacKenzie, A. Marshall and Alexander G.R. (Aberdeen and London)

Capitol Cinema (1933) (with David Stokes); All Saints Episcopal Church, Hilton, Aberdeen (1936); Jackson's Garage, Bon Accord Street, Aberdeen (1937); Northern Hotel, Aberdeen (1938); St Mary's Church, Aberdeen (1939); Aberdeen University Sports Pavilion, Aberdeen (1939-41).

McKissack, James (Glasgow)

1875-1940. Son of John McKissack (1844-1915), a prolific designer of churches for the Free Church of Scotland. James McKissack, in contrast, was a prolific cinema architect and also an accomplished cameraman. Eglinton Electreum, Eglinton Street, Glasgow (1911) +; La Scala, Sauchiehall Street, Glasgow (1912); Caley (alterations), Edinburgh (1927); Kingsway, Cathcart Road, Glasgow (1929); Broadway, Amulree Street, Glasgow (1930) +; un-built, Cumbernauld Road, Glasgow (1930); Hillhead Salon (alterations), Vinicombe Street, Glasgow (1931); Regal, Stranraer (1932) +; Mecca, Balmore Road, Glasgow (1933); Regal, Girvan (1933); Commodore, Dumbarton Road, Glasgow (1933) +; New Tivoli, Gorgie Road, Edinburgh (1934); Embassy, Pilton (1936) +; Vogue Dundee (1936) +; Raith, Kirkcaldy (1936); Embassy, Kilmarnock Road, Glasgow (1936) +; un-built, Hawthorn Street, Glasgow (1936); Grandstand, Shawfield Stadium, Glasgow (1936); Carlton, Piershill (1937) +; Embassy, Troon (1937) +; Tudor Cinema (alterations), Stockbridge, Edinburgh (1937) +; Vogue, Cumbernauld Road, Glasgow (1938); Vogue, Langlands Road, Govan, Glasgow (1938) +; Regal, Renfrew (alterations) (1938); Kyle, Irvine (1939) +; Cosmo,

Rose Street, Glasgow (1939); Boulevard (alterations), Knightscliffe Avenue, Glasgow (1939) +; Aldwych, Paisley Road West, Glasgow (1939) +. Work also included St Roch Roman Catholic School extension (1935).

McNair, Charles J. and Elder (Glasgow)

McNair, born 1881, licentiate of the RIBA. McNair got the work: Elder designed it. Primarily cinema designer. not short of 50 in number, 6 in 1939 alone. Paragon, Tobago Street, Glasgow (1910); un-built, Parliamentary Road, Glasgow (1910); Annfield (alterations), Gallowgate, Glasgow (1911) +; Cinema, Coburg Place, Glasgow (1911) +; Paladium, Dumbarton Road, Glasgow (1911) +; Palaceum, Edrom Street, Glasgow (1913) +; Cathcart Picture House, Old Castle Road, Glasgow (1913) +; Star (alterations), Dumbarton Road, Glasgow (1914) +; Royal Princess (alterations), Gorbals Street, Glasgow (1919); Western (alterations), Dumbarton Road, Glasgow (1919) +; Dennistoun Picture House, Armadale Street, Glasgow (1920) +; Western (alterations), Dumbarton Road, Glasgow (1921) +; Scotia, Millerston Street, Glasgow (1921) +; Dalmarnock, Nuneaton Street, Glasgow (1922) +; Lyric, Langlands Road, Glasgow (1922) +; un-built, Observatory Road, Glasgow (1922); Lyceum (alterations), Govan Road, Glasgow (1926) +; Blythswood, Maryhill Road, Glasgow (1927) +; Cambridge (alterations), New City Road, Glasgow (1927) +; Regal, Sauchiehall Street, Glasgow (1929); Rialto (alterations), Old Castle Road, Glasgow (1930) +; Lyceum (alterations), Govan Road, Glasgow (1930); Rex, Cumbernauld Road, Glasgow (1931) +; Regal, Hamilton (1931) +; Regal, Stirling (1932) +; Regal, Falkirk (1934); Regal, Paisley (1934); Gaiety (alterations), Argyle Street, Glasgow (1935) +; Palaceum (alterations), Edrom Street, Glasgow (1936) +; Plaza, Govan Road, Glasgow (1936) +; Plaza, Kilmarnock (1936) +; Regal, Coatbridge (1936); Rex, Motherwell (1936) +; Pavilion (alterations), Galashiels (1937); Princes, Gourlay Street, Glasgow (1937) +; State, Shettleston Road, Glasgow (1937) +; State, Castlemilk Road, Glasgow (1937) +; Regal, Kirkcaldy (1937); Olympia (alterations), Bridgeton Cross, Glasgow (1938); Lyceum, Govan Road, Glasgow (1938); Ascot, Great Western Road, Glasgow (1939) +. Also Dennistoun Palais (1937), Glen Moray Hotel, Dunoon (1937), extensions to Yarrow shipyard, Glasgow (1936), Ayr Old Church Session House and the Bellgrove Hotel, Duke Street, Glasgow.

Miller, James (Glasgow)

1860-1947. Pupil of Andrew Heiton, Perth. Promoted in Caledonian Railway civil engineering department and secured the confidence of its directors, co-designing several important stations, the most famous of which is Wemyss Bay. Full list of works exists in Royal Institute of Architects Scotland archive. Notable buildings include Hengler's Circus, Sauchiehall Street, Glasgow (1897) +; Savoy Theatre, Hope Street, Glasgow (1911) +; Cranston's Cinema De Luxe, Renfield Street, Glasgow (1916); Commercial Bank, Bothwell Street, Glasgow (1935); Perth Royal Infirmary extension (1931); Church of the Holy Rude. Stirling (1936); Greenock Hospital (1943); Canniesburn Hospital (1934); Larbert Colony (1936); Pavilion, South Beach (1937); and Lintwhite School (1900).

Naylor, R. and Sale, G.H. (Derby)

Initial house architects of Provincial Cinematograph Theatres. The Picture House, Dublin (1909), Manchester (1909), Birmingham (1910), Glasgow (1910 and 1912 re-build), Leicester (1910).

Paterson, Lennox D. (Hamilton)

Regal, Lanark (1936); the Regal, West Calder (1937) +; La Scala, Clydebank (1938); the Regal, Shotts (1939) +; the George, Bellshill (1951) +; re-builds of the Norwood, Glasgow (1952) and others for Associated G.P. Cinemas including the Crown, Gorbals, Glasgow (1953) + and the Picture House, Beith (1955) +.

Richardson, James S. (1883-1970) **and McKay, John Ross** (1884-1962) (Edinburgh)

Richardson was Inspector of Ancient Monuments for Scotland. His only cinema design was the Caley, Lothian Road, Edinburgh (1922-23) with McKay. The two also collaborated on Binn's Store, Princes Street, Edinburgh (1935).

Ross, Alexander and Son (Inverness)

Designer of numerous Church of Scotland and Episcopal churches. Also Inverness Market and Arcade (1870); alterations to Cawdor and Skibo Castles and a number of hotels. The Central Picture House, Inverness (1912) +, designed by Ross' son, Alister, was the firm's only cinema design.

Stellmac & Co (Building Contractors)

Builders of a number of near-identical small-town cinemas in the mid- to late-1930s. Ritz, Newton-on-Ayr; Ritz, Camelon +; Ritz, Lesmahagow +; Regal, Dalry +; Picture House, Dalbeattie and New Cumnock Picture House (alterations) +.

Stokes, David (Aberdeen and London)

Graduated from Architectural Association in 1930. Set up with P. Fleetwood-Hesketh. 1933: firm closed with no work. A. G. R. MacKenzie offered the design partnership in Aberdeen to replace Clement George who had died. He worked on the Capitol Cinema, the Stuart House in Banchory and Halifax Building Society offices in Union Street. According to Charles McKean's *The Scottish Thirties*, glad to return to London in 1935.

Sutherland, Eric A. (Glasgow)

1870-1940. Various Savings Banks in Glasgow including Hillhead (1939) and High Street, Ayr (1935-37). Designer of Govanhill Picture House, Bankhall Street, Glasgow (1926); Mayfair Cinema, Sinclair Drive, Glasgow (1933) +; La Scala, Dunoon (1936).

Sutherland, T. Scott (Aberdeen)

1899-1963. Graduate of Robert Gordon's College and Gray's School of Art. One-legged but expert bridge player, stalwart Aberdeen Magical Society, fine swimmer, tennis player, cricketer and fisherman. 1934: stood as Progressive candidate in Ruthrieston by-election. At height of election had 80 cars ferrying voters to polling station. Spent £59 on his election – local paper noted the highest sum for a number of years. Was elected and became Housing Convener. Responsible for Kincorth Housing Competition (1936). Founder director of Caledonian Associated Cinemas. Director of 39 other companies including Silver City Lido, Tivoli Theatre Company, Inverurie Pictures Ltd, Aberdeen Varieties Ltd, chairman James Allan and Company Furnishers. Branch manager and architect for Scottish Amicable, director of Modern Homes (Aberdeen), chairman Dunblane Hydro, promoter of Aberdeen Ice Rink. Buildings include Broomhill Estate, bungalows, Poole's Regent Cinema, Aberdeen (1932); Astoria Cinema, Kittybrewster (1935) +; Victoria Cinema, Inverurie (1936); Majestic Cinema, Union Street, Aberdeen (1937) +; Playhouse, Peterhead (1937); Dunblane Hydro Hotel refurbishment and Hazelhead Clubhouse.

Swanston, John D. (Kirkcaldy)

1869-1956. A Kirkcaldy architect and town councillor who produced designs for several fine Edwardian theatres, such as the King's Theatres in Kirkcaldy (1904) and Edinburgh (1906); The Empire, Cowdenbeath (1899) +; Gaiety, Methil (1907); the Palace, Kirkcaldy (1913) +; the Alexandra in Belfast (1911) + and a new interior for the Dunfermline Opera House (1921) +.

Thomson, James (Dundee)

1904-24 Dundee City Architect and Engineer. King's Theatre, Dundee (1909); Caird Hall, Dundee (1914-22).

Trent, William E. (London)

House architect to Provincial Cinematograph Theatres and, later, to Gaumont-British Cinemas. In Scotland, New Victoria, Edinburgh (1930); Gaumont, Alloa (1939).

Unick Architects (formerly Howard & Unick) (Glasgow)

Prolific designers of generic multiplex cinemas. The firm works internationally, yet maintains a low profile.

Verity, Frank T. (d. 1937) **and Beverley, Samuel** (London)

Fashionable London-based firm. 1930s cinema projects designed by Beverley. Having designed Paramount's flagship Plaza in London's Lower Regent Street (1926) and the Carlton Theatre in nearby Haymarket (1927), the firm went on to design a number of Paramounts in Britain's provincial cities, commencing with Manchester (1930). Beverley also designed large and luxuriously-appointed cinemas for Union Cinemas in England only. The Paramount, Glasgow (1934) was the firm's only Scottish work.

Watson, John (1873-1936), **Salmond, David** (1876-1938) **and Gray, James H.** (1885-1938) (Glasgow)

Davidson Hospital, Girvan (1921); Waverley, Shawlands, Glasgow (1922); Glasgow City Chambers extension (1923).

Caledonian Associated Cinemas was the largest Scottish-headquartered circuit. The Playhouse in Gordon Street, Huntly (opened in 1932) was typical of their smaller properties. (Bruce Peter collection)

The 1934 Playhouse in Argyll Square, Oban was one of several Scottish cinemas to succumb to fire – a hazard caused largely by the number of people who smoked. (Bruce Peter collection)

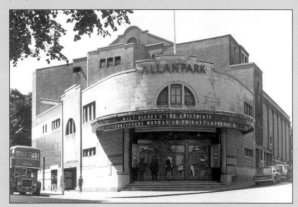

The Allanpark in Stirling (Sam Runcie, 1938) was built for Stirling Cinema & Variety Theatres Ltd and acquired by CAC in 1969. It continued as a combined cinema and bingo club until 2008. (Tony Moss collection, CTA Archive)

In Dalkeith, near Edinburgh, CAC's Playhouse and Pavilion cinemas stood next door to one another in the town's Buccleuch Street. The Playhouse dated from the mid-1930s. The Pavilion was of older vintage. (Tony Moss collection, CTA Archive)

Above: CAC's 678-seat Playhouse in Fort William dated from 1931. It became a bingo hall in 1978 but has since been demolished. (Bruce Peter collection)

Left: CAC regarded the Regal, Dunfermline (T. Bowhill Gibson, 1931) as a flagship property, second only to their Perth Playhouse. The cinema's façade had Egyptian overtones, a briefly fashionable aesthetic for commercial buildings following the discovery of King Tutankhamun's tomb. (Bruce Peter collection)

Important Figures in the Cinema Exhibition Business in Scotland

Bendon, Prince (Glasgow) One of the pioneers of the industry, both on the exhibiting and renting sides. In addition to being the proprietor of the Bendon Trading Co., he founded and became president of the Glasgow Cinema Club and also served as president of the Royal Clyde Motor Yacht Club. For six years, he was president of the Scottish Kinematograph Renters' Society.

Bennell, Ritson (Glasgow) Commercial training in office organisation and equipment business with Kenrick & Jefferson Ltd. Joined Trade in 1912 as buyer for BB Pictures, subsequently took charge of BB Picture Renting interests. After leaving the Army had renting experience with Goldwyn and Gaumont Co, and rejoined BB Pictures in 1926 as managing director. Joined Gaumont-British 1929 and became supervisor of the Corporation's interests in Scotland.

Cartlidge, William (London) General manager, Associated British Cinemas; born May 1910. Joined ABC as manager, 1933; appointed general manager of company, March 1951.

Deutsch, Oscar (Birmingham and London) Born 1893 in Birmingham. Chairman and governing director of the Odeon Circuit. Entered the industry on the renting side, being chairman of W. & F. Film Service (Midlands) Ltd, for several years. Entered exhibiting side in 1925, but it was not until 1933 that he commenced building up the Odeon circuit.

Green, Herbert J. (Glasgow) A principal in George Green Circuit; hon. treasurer, Scottish Branch CEA.; president and treasurer, Scottish Cinema and Theatre Benevolent Fund ; son of the late George Green; the Green Circuit, in which he and his brother were associated, included Green's Playhouse, Renfield Street, Glasgow (seating 4,235), the largest cinema in Europe when first opened; Green's Playhouse, Dundee (seating 4,150) ; Green's Playhouse, Ayr (seating 3,300) and Green's Playhouse, Wishaw (seating 3,000).

Grove, Brigadier I. R. (Queensferry, West Lothian) Entered the cinema trade in 1911. Managing director, FTS (Great Britain) Ltd; London and Provincial Film Transport Co Ltd; Lothians Star Theatres Ltd; Star Theatre (Lochore) Ltd; Primrose Pictures Ltd; director, Glasgow and West of Scotland Cinemas Ltd; Grove Picture Houses (Glasgow) Ltd; Astoria Cinemas (Glasgow) Ltd; Arbroath Picture House Co

Ltd; first commandant, Army Kineum Services, 1941; deputy director, War Office, 1943-44; first director, Inter-services Kinematography, India, 1944-46; latterly chief technical adviser to Army Kine Corporation and member of the board of management.

Kemp, Harry (Ardrossan) Born 1912, Johnstone, Renfrewshire; son of showman George Kemp. In the 1930s, Kemp operated a Saltcoats-based circuit consisting of La Scala and the Regal, Saltcoats and the Grange, Stevenston. Later, the firm invested in amusement arcades.

King, Sir Alexander B. (Glasgow) Born 1888. First entered the cinema business at the age of 12; Cinema Exhibitors Association President, 1949/50; member of the Cinematograph Films Council; Honorary Treasurer, Scottish Tourist Board; knighted 1944.

McLaughlin, Robert (Edinburgh) Born 1898; entered the cinema industry 1923; director and general manager of the Caley Picture House Co, director and secretary, Cinema Properties Ltd; Cinema Holdings (Kirkcaldy) Ltd; Inveresk Cinema Co Ltd; East Fife Cinema Co Ltd; Raith Cinema Co Ltd; Granton Cinema Co Ltd; Thornliebuk Cinema Co Ltd; Sighthill Cinema Co Ltd; Leith Cinema Co Ltd; Kinnear Morison, Ltd; chairman Scottish branch Cinema Exhibitors Association, 1934.

Maxwell, John (Glasgow and London) Born 1877. Entered the film business in 1912 as an exhibitor, subsequently developing Scottish Cinema and Variety Theatres into a substantial regional circuit. Later he became involved with Wardour Films Ltd and, as chairman of that company, did much to make it the foremost independent renting business in the trade. Next, he turned his attention to film production and was the moving light in the creation of British International Pictures Ltd. Chairman and managing director, Associated British Picture Corporation Ltd. His Associated British Cinemas circuit was Britain's largest by the end of the 1930s.

Milne, John B. (Dundee) Born 1902. Entered industry as kine-variety violinist; purchased Palladium, Dundee in 1928; controlled 19 cinemas, including halls in Lewis and the Shetland Isles.

Ostrer, Isidore (London) Chairman, Lothbury Investment Corporation Ltd. and Premier Productions Ltd; up to 1941 chairman of Gaumont-British Picture Corporation Ltd.

Ostrer, Mark (London) Director, Gaumont-British Picture Corporation Ltd and Gaumont-British Distributors Ltd; originally a merchant banker; with his brothers, Isidore and Maurice, took financial interest in Gaumont Co Ltd, 1922; active in formation of Gaumont-British Picture Corporation Ltd; also joint managing director of Provincial Cinematograph Theatres Ltd and General Theatres Corporation Ltd; director Denman Picture Houses Ltd.

Palmer, George (Glasgow) Born 1903; educated at Govan High School and Glasgow Technical College. Managing director, Associated G.P. Cinemas Ltd, Associated G.P. Cinemas (Finance) Ltd, Associated G.P. Cinemas (Caterers) Ltd, Associated G.P. Cinemas (Accessories) Ltd.

Pickard, Albert E. (Glasgow) 1880-1966. An immigrant from London who became notorious as a property speculator and who claimed millionaire status by the 1930s. Pickard was also involved in the entertainment business, purchasing the Britannia Music Hall in Glasgow's Trongate and re-opening it as the Panopticon in 1899 with cinema and variety. Pickard went on to develop a small chain of cinemas of dubious quality in and around Glasgow and one in Clydebank. His Glasgow venues were sold to the A.B. King circuit in 1935.

Poole, John R. (Edinburgh) The Pooles were a family from Gloucester who presented Diorama shows in the pre-cinema era, visiting Edinburgh as they toured the country. John R. Poole later settled in Edinburgh, where he expanded the company's cinema circuit to two venues in Edinburgh (the Synod Hall and the Roxy) and two in Aberdeen (the Palace and the Regent). His Aberdeen venues passed to County Cinemas in the early-1930s and, later, to Odeon.

Priest, Lionel F. (Bathgate) Director and general manager, Lothians Star Theatres, Bathgate, since 1943 ; general manager and supervisor, Star Theatre (Lochore) Ltd; director, Arbroath Cinema Co Ltd; Picture House, Stewarton, Ayrshire; member of Edinburgh section of CEA since entering trade; East of Scotland representative on general council, and chairman, Scottish branch, 1950.

Rank, J. Arthur (London) Born 1888; educated at Leys School, Cambridge. Chairman of Odeon Theatres Ltd, Gaumont-British Picture Corporation Ltd, British and Dominions Film Corporation Ltd, General Cinema Finance Corporation Ltd, J. Arthur Rank Organisation Ltd., Circuits Management Association Ltd. Chairman and managing director of Joseph Rank Ltd; director, Eagle Star Insurance Company Ltd.

Scott, George Urie (Glasgow) Recognised as one of the pioneers of the industry. Began in 1908 as an exhibitor and gradually acquired a circuit of seven theatres in Scotland. In addition to being president of the Cinema Club, Glasgow, he was a president of the Scottish Branch of the Cinema Exhibitors Association.

Singleton, George (Glasgow) Born 1900; managing director Singleton Cinemas Ltd; director Scottish Repertory Cinemas Ltd; governor, Scottish Film Council. Chairman of the Scottish Branch of the Cinema Exhibitors Association.

Taylor, George (Glasgow) General manager George Taylor circuit; chairman, Scottish Branch of the Cinema Exhibitors Association, 1953-54.

Welsh, James (Glasgow) Born 1881. Served as Member of Parliament for Paisley in the 1929-31 period and subsequently became Glasgow's Lord Provost between 1943 and 1945. Long experience of Local Government work. Entered the industry in 1910 as exhibitor. Active in the Cinema Exhibitors Association since its formation.

Important Scottish Cinema Circuits

+ Indicates that the cinema has been entirely demolished

Associated British Cinemas Ltd (London)
1939

Regal, Aberdeen (under construction) +
Palace, Arbroath +
Ritz, Cambuslang +
Bank, Clydebank +
Empire, Clydebank +
Regal, Coatbridge
Rialto, Dumbarton
Regal, Dumfries
Plaza, Dundee +
Lyceum, Edinburgh +
Regal, Edinburgh +
Ritz, Edinburgh +
Savoy, Stockbridge, Edinburgh +
Picture House, Falkirk
Regal, Falkirk
Playhouse, Galashiels
Coliseum, Glasgow +
Grosvenor, Hillhead, Glasgow
Mayfair, Battlefield, Glasgow +
Olympia, Bridgeton, Glasgow
Picture House, Dennistoun, Glasgow +
Picture House. Govanhill, Glasgow
Picture Palace, Parkhead, Glasgow +
Plaza, Govan, Glasgow +
Princess, Springburn, Glasgow +
Regal, Glasgow
Rex, Riddrie, Glasgow +
Rhul, Burnside, Glasgow +
Ritz, Oatlands, Glasgow +
Toledo, Muirend, Glasgow
Waverley, Shawlands, Glasgow
Regal, Greenock +
Regal, Hamilton +
Tower, Helensburgh +
George Picture House, Kilmarnock
Regal, Kilmarnock
Regal, Kirkcaldy
King's, Montrose
La Scala, Motherwell +
Rex, Motherwell +
Regal, Paisley +
Regal, Stirling +
Plaza, Wishaw +

Associated G.P. Cinemas (Glasgow)
1955

Victory, Whiteinch, Glasgow +
George, Largs
Viking, Largs +
George, Cathcart, Glasgow +
Eastway, Edinburgh +
Regal, Girvan
George, Glasgow
George, Irvine +
George, Beith +
George, Crown Street, Glasgow +
George, Bellshill +
Alhambra, Bellshill +
Victory, Portobello +
George, Portobello
George, Uddingston +
George, Troon +
Palace, Irvine +
George, Kilbirnie
Regal, Mossend +

Caledonian Associated Cinemas Ltd (Inverness)
1955

Cinema, Brodick
Playhouse, Callander
Cinema, Crieff
Playhouse, Dunbar +
Picture House, Elgin
Playhouse, Elgin
Picture House, Grantown-on-Spey
La Scala, Grangemouth
Playhouse, Invergordon
Playhouse, Innerleithen +
Empire Theatre, Inverness +
La Scala, Inverness +
Playhouse, Inverness +
Playhouse, Keith
Playhouse, Montrose +
Kelburne Cinema, Paisley +
Playhouse, Peebles
Playhouse, Perth
Playhouse, Peterhead
Cinema, Lamlash, Arran
Avondale, Strathaven +
Ritz, Strathaven
Picture House, Tain
Picture House, Thurso +

The 1,228-seat Astoria in Edinburgh's Corstorphine district (T. Bowhill Gibson, 1930) served a rapidly expanding suburb. It continued until 1974 when it was demolished in favour of a supermarket – an instance of one fashionable building type being replaced by another. (Tony Moss collection, CTA Archive)

The Cinema House in Bathgate's Livery Street was converted from an ice rink in 1913. Regarded as being the least salubrious of the town's three cinemas, it was also the first to close and it subsequently became a dance hall in the 1960s. (Tony Moss collection, CTA Archive)

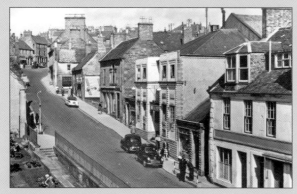

The King's in Brechin's High Street opened in 1927 and film shows continued until 1985. In market towns serving large agricultural hinterlands, cinemas were popular amenities.

(Bruce Peter collection)

La Scala in Hamilton (James McKissack, 1921) initially belonged to the local Thomas Ormiston circuit. Gaumont-British purchased this in 1928 and the cinema was eventually renamed the Gaumont in 1950. (Bruce Peter collection)

The Regal in Bonnyrigg, East Lothian, was converted in the mid-1930s from the 1913-vintage Picture House.

(Bruce Peter collection)

The Savoy in Cambuslang (John Fairweather, 1929) was solidly constructed and remains remarkably intact, having served until recently as a bingo hall. Here, it is seen in the 1950s. (Bruce Peter collection)

Cinema, Whiting Bay
Breadalbane Hall, Wick +
Pavilion, Wick +
Playhouse, Fort William +
Playhouse, Fraserburgh
Picture House, Fraserburgh
Playhouse, Buckie
Playhouse, Huntly +
Regal, Lossiemouth
Playhouse, Nairn
Picture House, Kingussie
Palace, Rothesay +
Regal, Rothesay +
Palace, Rosyth
Ritz, Rothesay
Regal, Dunfermline +
Mosspark Picture House, Glasgow +
Rio, Bearsden, Glasgow +
Rio, Kirkcaldy +
Rio, Rutherglen +
Playhouse, Dalkeith
Pavilion, Dalkeith
Empire, Dunbar +
Empire, Linlithgow +
Playhouse, North Berwick +
Empire, Peebles +
Playhouse, Penicuik

J.F. Donald (Aberdeen Picture Palaces Ltd and Aberdeen Cinema Ltd) (Aberdeen)
1953

Astoria, Kittybrewster, Aberdeen +
Capitol, Union Street, Aberdeen
Cinema House, Skene Terrace, Aberdeen
City, George Street, Aberdeen +
Grand Central, George Street, Aberdeen +
His Majesty's Theatre, Union Terrace, Aberdeen
Kingsway, King Street, Aberdeen
Majestic, Union Street, Aberdeen +
Playhouse, Union Street, Aberdeen +
Queen's Cinema, Union Street, Aberdeen
Torry Cinema, Cromlie Road, Aberdeen +

Gaumont-British Picture Corporation Ltd and associated companies (London)
1939

Denman Picture Houses Ltd
La Scala, Alloa (demolished and replaced by Gaumont)
Gaumont, Alloa
Picture House, Ayr +
Picture Theatre, Bellshill

BB Picture House, Coatbridge +
Pavilion, Falkirk +
Florida, Glasgow +
BB Cinema, Glasgow +
Parade Picture House, Dennistoun, Glasgow +
Capitol, Ibrox, Glasgow +
New Savoy, Glasgow +
Tivoli, Partick, Glasgow +
La Scala, Hamilton
Rialto, Kirkcaldy +
Pavilion, Kirkintilloch +
Pavilion, Motherwell +
Alhambra, Perth +
BB Cinerama, Perth +
Cinema, Wishaw

General Theatre Corporation Ltd
Regent Picture House, Edinburgh +
Rutland Picture House, Edinburgh +
Picture House, St. Andrew's Square, Edinburgh +
Capitol, Leith

United Picture Theatres Ltd
King's Theatre, Dundee
New Picture House, Edinburgh +
New Victoria, Edinburgh
Picture House, Glasgow +
Picture House, Aberdeen +

George Green Ltd (Glasgow)
1939

Playhouse, Ayr
Pavilion, Bathgate
Rex Cinema, Campbeltown +
Playhouse, Dundee. +
La Scala, Dunoon
New Bedford, Glasgow
Picturedrome, Gorbals, Glasgow +
Playhouse, Renfield Street, Glasgow +
Strathclyde Cinema, Glasgow +
Cinema, Tollcross, Glasgow +
Green's, Irvine
Pavilion, Johnstone +
Cinema, Rutherglen +
Playhouse, Wishaw
Rex, Lockerbie

Sir A.B. King Circuit (Glasgow)
1955

(In addition, King booked films for the Caledonian
Associated Cinemas circuit and sat on CAC's board)

Cinema, Airdrie +
Strand, Alexandria +
Orient, Ayr
Ritz, Ayr
Hippodrome, Bo'ness
Central, Broxburn +
La Scala, Clydebank
Cinema, Coatbridge +
Lyceum, Dumfries +
Astoria, Glasgow +
Cambridge Cinema, Glasgow +
Casino, Townhead, Glasgow +
Elder Picture House, Govan, Glasgow +
Elephant, Shawlands, Glasgow
Embassy, Shawlands, Glasgow +
Gaiety, Anderston, Glasgow +
Hampden, Crosshill, Glasgow +
La Scala, Glasgow +
Lorne Cinema, Ibrox, Glasgow +
Lyceum, Govan, Glasgow
New Grand, Cowcaddens, Glasgow +
Regent, Glasgow +
Rosevale, Glasgow
Seamore, Glasgow +
Carlton, Glasgow +
Roxy, Maryhill, Glasgow +
Standard, Partick +
Avon, Possilpark +
Astor, Springburn +
BB Cinema, Greenock
La Scala, Helensburgh
Empire, Kilmarnock +
Plaza, Kilmarnock +
Regal, Lanark
La Scala, Paisley +
Plaza, Port Glasgow
Broadway Cinema , Prestwick
Cinema, St. Andrews +
Countess Cinema, Saltcoats

Lothians Star Theatres (Bathgate)
1939

Star, Armadale +
Regal, Armadale +
Cinema House, Bathgate +
Regal, Bathgate
Star, Bo'ness
Regal, Broxburn +
Regal, Shotts +
Regal, West Calder +

J. B. Milne Theatres (Dundee)
1955

Regal, Auchterarder
Regal, Blairgowrie +
Ritz, Crieff
La Scala, Cupar +
Picture House, Cowdenbeath +
Alhambra, Dunfermline
Kinnaird, Dundee +
Broadway Theatre, Dundee +
Rex, Dundee +
Regal Cinema, Dundee +
Victoria Theatre, Dundee +
County, Kinross +
Opera House, Lochgelly +
Regal, Macduff
Palace, Methil +
Regal, Peterhead
Picture House, Banff.
Playhouse, Stornoway +
North Star, Lerwick +
Gray's, Dundee +
Rialto, Dundee +
Astoria, Dundee +

Odeon Theatres Ltd (London)
1939

Pavilion Picture House, Airdrie +
Odeon Theatre, Ayr
Odeon Theatre, Coatbridge +
Empire Theatre, Dundee +
Odeon Theatre, Dundee +
Cinema, Falkirk +
Paragon Theatre, Glasgow +
Odeon Theatre, Glasgow
Odeon Theatre, Scotstoun, Glasgow +
Odeon Theatre, Shettleston, Glasgow +
Odeon Theatre, Hamilton +
King's Cinema, Hawick +
Odeon Theatre, Motherwell +
Odeon Theatre, Rutherglen

George Urie Scott Circuit (Glasgow)
1939

Cathcart Picture Playhouse Ltd
State Cinema, Shettleston, Glasgow +
State Cinema, King's Park, Glasgow +

Anderston Pictures and Varieties Ltd
New Gaiety Cinema, Anderston, Glasgow +

Scott Theatres Ltd
Palaceum, Shettleston, Glasgow +
Empire, Larkhall +
Pavilion, Barrhead +
Pavilion, Hawick +
Theatre, Hawick +

Singleton Cinemas Ltd (Glasgow)
1935

Pavilion Picture House, Airdrie +
Premier Pictures, Bridgeton, Glasgow +
Plaza, Burnbank, Hamilton +
Commodore, Scotstoun, Glasgow +
Empire, Coatbridge +
Cinema, Falkirk +
Paragon, Glasgow +
Empire, Dundee +
King's, Hawick +
Broadway, Shettleston, Glasgow +

1955
Vogue, Knightswood, Glasgow +
Vogue, Govan, Glasgow +
Vogue, Possilpark, Glasgow
Aldwych, Glasgow +
Vogue, Riddrie, Glasgow
Kingsway, Cathcart, Glasgow +
Westway, Glasgow +
Plaza, Burnbank, Hamilton +
Cosmo, Glasgow

George Taylor Circuit (Glasgow)
1955

New Partick Picture House, Glasgow +
Kelvin, Glasgow +
New Star, Glasgow +
West End, Paisley +
New Alex, Paisley +
Picture House, Dunoon +
Orient, Glasgow +

Bibliography

Atwell, David and McKean, Charles, Battle of Styles: London 1914-1939, RIBA, London, 1973.

Atwell, David, Cathedrals of the Movies, The Architectural Press, London, 1981.

Baacke, Rolf-Peter, Lichtspielhausarchitektur in Deutschland, Verlag Frolich & Kaufmann, Hamburg, 1982.

Banham, Mary and Hillier, Bevis (eds), A Tonic To The Nation: The Festival of Britain 1951, Thames & Hudson, London, 1976.

Barnes, John, The Beginnings of the Cinema in England, David & Charles, Newton Abbot, 1976.

Clegg, Rosemary, Odeon, Mercia Cinema Society Publications, 1985.

McLaren Young, Andrew and Doak, A.M., Glasgow at a Glance, Collins, Glasgow, 1965.

Eyles, Allen, ABC: The First Name In Entertainment, BFI Publishing, London, 1993.

Eyles, Allen, Gaumont-British Cinemas, BFI Publishing, London, 1996.

Eyles, Allen, The Granada Theatres, BFI Publishing, London, 1998.

Eyles, Allen and Skone, Keith, London's West End Cinemas, Keystone, Surbiton, 1984.

Gray, Richard, Cinemas of Britain: One Hundred Years of Cinema Architecture, Lund Humphries, London, 1996.

Hall, Ben M., The Best Remaining Seats: The Story of the Golden Age of the Movie Palace, Bramhall House, New York, 1961.

High, David, The First Hundred Years: The Story of the Empire, Leicester Square, Amber Valley, Birmingham, 1985.

Ind, Rosemary, Emberton, London & Berkeley Scolar Press, 1983.

Jackson, Anthony, The Politics of Architecture: A History of Modern Architecture in Britain, The Architectural Press, London, 1970.

Kenna, Rudolph, Glasgow Art Deco, Richard Drew, Glasgow, 1985.

Kinchin, Perilla and Juliet, Glasgow's Great Exhibitions 1888-1901-1911-1938-1988, White Cockade, Wendlebury, Oxon, 1988.

McBain, Janet, Pictures Past, Moorfoot, Edinburgh, 1984.

Mackintosh, Iain and Sell, Michael, Curtains!!! Or A New Life for Old Theatres, John Offord, Eastbourne, 1982.

McKean, Charles, The Scottish Thirties, Scottish Academic Press, Edinburgh, 1987.

Naylor, David, American Picture Palaces: The Architecture of Fantasy, Prentice Hall Press, Washington D.C., 1981.

Peter, Bruce, Glasgow's Amazing Cinemas, Polygon, Glasgow, 1996.

Richards, Jeffrey, The Age of the Dream Palace: Cinema and Society in Britain 1930-1939, Routledge & Kegan Paul, London, 1984.

Richards, J.M., The Castles on the Ground, Piper, London, 1948.

Shand, P. Morton, Modern Theatres and Cinemas, Batsford, London, 1930.

Sharp, Dennis, The Picture Palace and Other Buildings for the Movies, Hugh Evelyn Ltd, London, 1969.

Smith, Terry, Making the Modern: Industry, Art and Design in America, Chicago University Press, Chicago, 1993.

Stephan, Regina (Ed), Eric Mendelsohn Architect 1887-1953, The Monacelli Press, New York, 2000.

Thomas, Michael, Silver Screen in the Silver City: A History of Cinemas in Aberdeen 1896-1987, Aberdeen University Press, 1988.

EXHIBITION CATALOGUES

Brave New Worlds, The Glasgow School of Art, Glasgow, 1999.

International Architecture 1924-1934, RIBA, London, 1934.

Peto, James and Loveday, Donna (eds), Modern Britain 1929-1939, The Design Museum, London, 1999.

WEBSITES

www.scottishcinemas.org

NEWSPAPERS AND PERIODICALS

ABC News

The Aberdeen Press and Journal

Architecture Illustrated

The Architect and Building News

The Architect's Journal

Architectural Design and Construction

The Architectural Record

The Architectural Review

The Bailie

The Builder and Construction Weekly

Building Industries

Cinema and Theatre Construction

Cinemas, Theatres and Ballrooms

The Dunfermline Press

The Evening News

Focus on Film

The Glasgow Herald

The Glasgow Weekly Programme

The Ideal Kinema

Milden Miscellany

Picture House

Prospect Magazine

The Quiz

RIAS Quarterly

RIBA Journal

The Scotsman

The Scottish Field

SMT Scottish Country Life

The Theatres Trust Newsletter

The Times

Index